Behind Latticed Marble

Inner Worlds of Women

Jyotirmoyee Devi Sen

Translated from Bengali by **Apala G. Egan**

NIYOGI BOOKS

Published by
NIYOGI BOOKS
Block D, Building No. 77,
Okhla Industrial Area, Phase-I,
New Delhi-110 020, INDIA
Tel: 91-11-26816301, 26818960
Email: niyogibooks@gmail.com
Website: www.niyogibooksindia.com

English Text © Apala G. Egan

Editor: Arunima Ghosh
Design: Shashi Bhushan Prasad
Cover Design: Misha Oberoi

ISBN: 978-93-91125-33-2
Publication: 2023

This is a work of fiction. The names, characters and incidents portrayed in it are the work of the author's imagination. Any resemblance to actual persons, living or dead, events or localities, is entirely coincidental.

All rights are reserved. No part of this publication may be reproduced or transmitted in any form or by any means, electronic or mechanical, including photocopying, recording or by any information storage and retrieval system without prior written permission and consent of the Publisher.

Printed at: Niyogi Offset Pvt. Ltd., New Delhi, India

CONTENTS

Introduction	5
Beneath the Aravalli Hills	13
first published in Saint Ann's Review, *USA*	
Frame-Up	32
first published in Talking River, *USA*	
The Child Bride	54
first published in The Missouri Review, *USA*	
The Queen and the Concubine	90
first published in Ellery Queen Mystery Magazine, *USA*	
The Taint	104
first published in South Carolina Review, *USA*	
Ungendered	124
first published in Xavier Review, *USA*	
The Courtesan's Tale	145
first published in Istanbul Review, *Turkey*	
The Mistress Wife	165
first published in Catamaran Literary Reader, *USA*	
The Princess Baby	183
first published in the J Journal, *USA*	
Two Women	198
first published in Talking River, *USA*	
Acknowledgments	215

INTRODUCTION

The stories should be viewed in the context of human history and that of women in particular. In these pages I have provided a quick overview of women's history and highlighted only a few regions and notable women.

To many ancient peoples, the earth was the source of sustenance. The belief in the sacredness of life-giving water at the sources of rivers and springs began in prehistory. Greek, Roman, Celtic and Baltic tales speak of female spiritual figures connected with water. Thus, many ancient cultures believed in the Feminine Principle and had a deep regard for nature as the creator of life. Some of these societies achieved a high level of aristic skill. Beautiful pieces of pottery have been discovered by archeologists in Anatolia, Turkey and in parts of Europe. Invasions by nomadic groups led to the destruction of some of these societies.

Some societies escaped the path of invasions for a while, due to their location. There were indeed ancient civilizations which worshipped the Goddess and lived in harmony with nature. One such example is Crete, also referred to as

Minoan Crete, after King Minos. Archeologists discovered an advanced culture with well-organized cities, palaces, villas and granaries. The frescoes and carvings were fine and delicate and drew their inspiration from the environment. Images of warfare tended to be absent in their artwork, and men and women lived in harmony while honoring the earth and reaping its bounties.

Another example from around that time would be that of the Harappan civilization in the Indian subcontinent that extends from the northwest all the way down to Gujarat. Large, meticulously planned cities with homes and buildings and an elaborate drainage system existed. The people were skilled metal workers as the jewelry and artifacts indicate. According to archeologists, they also worshipped a mother goddess and lived in harmony with their surroundings.

In certain regions of the world and at different times, women of wisdom and learning have thrived. Around three thousand years ago, in the Indian subcontinent, a woman philosopher named Maitreyi contributed hymns to the *Rig Veda*, a sacred text. In Tibet, Machig Lapdron is one of the most renowned and beloved of Tibetan mystics. Born about a thousand years ago, she showed extraordinary intelligence as a child and her parents encouraged her education. She went for further learning at a monastery and a whole body of teachings is credited to her.

With the spread of warfare in various parts of the world, and a patriarchal form of existence, the practice of plural marriages arose for political and social reasons. The Bible mentions that King Solomon had wives and concubines; in Europe among the royalty throughout history, kings routinely kept mistresses. It is in this context that we need to view the author's stories; the writer, on a number of occasions, had the opportunity to visit the royal palaces with her family.

Violence also arose against women in certain patriarchal belief systems. The women-centered, old spiritual traditions celebrating nature, traditional healing and creativity were deemed as evil. The witch hunt from the 15th to the 18th centuries conducted by the Christian Church in Europe led to the mass murder of countless women. Those who were traditional healers, and poor country women, if single or widowed, were particularly vulnerable. In Brahmanical Hinduism, over the centuries, the immolation of widows from certain castes and classes, regardless of age, occurred. This particular practice was defined as sati.

With the ascendance of male-dominated cultures, some women were relegated to the role of entertainers. In ancient Greece, *hetaerae* were women who were trained in music, dance and speech, and provided entertainment for men. In Japan, the role of the *geisha* was similar, but more secluded. In historic India, courtesans were talented dancers and singers, and performed for wealthy men. A famous example is the courtesan, Amrapali, who lived about two and half thousand years ago. Upon meeting the Buddha and hearing his sermons, she decided to become a nun. In the author's stories, female performers, however, were exclusively part of the palace entourage.

In ancient Greece, some young girls captured in battle were chosen to become *hetaerae* if they were beautiful; sometimes, impoverished parents might also sell their good-looking daughters. Likewise, in the writer's stories, poor village folk might try to sell or give their daughters to the palace.

During the age of empires, where women's roles may have been somewhat circumscribed, ladies of royalty and nobility were great patrons of the arts and architecture. Queen Devi, wife of Emperor Ashoka, built the famed Sanchi Stupa in Madhya Pradesh, India, and founded a monastery there, over two thousand years ago. The exquisite carvings on the gates and pillars show details of the Buddha's life as well as that of ordinary folk. Her daughter, Sanghamitra, and son, Mahendra, went to SriLanka to spread his teachings.

Virupaksha Temple, also known as Lokeshwara Temple, in Karnataka, India, was built over a thousand years ago by Queen Lokamahadevi. Carved out of red sandstone, stories from the Hindu epics are etched on the walls, pillars and niches.

Rani Rashmoni, a woman of noble birth, built the elaborate Dakshineswar Kali Temple in Bengal, India, around the middle of the 19th century.

In Europe, Marie Antoinette, queen of France in the 18th century, supported women artists such as Elisabeth Louise Vigée Le Brun for her skill in painting portraits. Madame de Pompadour, mistress to King Louis XV of France, helped shape artistic taste in 18th-century France. In the field of interior design, that era is known as the rococo period where the focus of décor was more delicate, light and graceful.

Philanthropy was another area where women excelled, even in societies where their public role was limited. In Japan, Lady Takeko Kujo founded the Asoka Hospital, one of Japan's first modern medical centers. She died in Tokyo after contracting an illness during her work in the city's slums, following a major earthquake.

Rajput men, the author states in her memoirs, were chivalrous and considered it a mark of honor to help their *behen-beti* (sisters and daughters), and this generosity extended to women of all races and classes. The royal government provided daily meals to the destitute. Food baskets consisting of grains, fruits and vegetables, and even spending cash, were granted to those especially hard-hit, such as widowed womenfolk. The queens and queen mothers too, had their own private charities. Indigent women, in addition to food baskets, received nourishing milk-based puddings from the queens' personal kitchens. Members of the royal family were devotees of Sri Govindji (Sri Krishna) and his consort Sree Radha Ladliji Devi, and provided support and aid to local temples as well.

The writer's stories and memoirs describe royal women as being patrons of the arts. Queens had their own dance troupes and would organize performances at palace festivities to which certain members of the community were invited. Royal ladies often showed a keen interest in artistic work and the décor of the palace interiors.

During the 19th century in Bengal, the leading men of society began questioning some of the pernicious customs such as sati. Rammohun Roy campaigned for its abolition, and he, along with Swami Vivekananda and Ishwar Chandra Vidyasagar among others, spearheaded major religious and social reform movements. This period is referred to as the Bengal Renaissance, but it had far-reaching effects in the Indian subcontinent as well. In this milieu, some families, while still adhering to the custom of early betrothal, encouraged the education of their daughters at the hands of private tutors, as was the case with the author.

There are unique links between Keshub Chandra Sen, a key figure in this era, and the Rajput kingdom. His brother, Harimohan Sen, designed the beautiful city gardens and museums in Jaipur. Keshub Chandra Sen's daughter, Suniti

Devi, married the Maharaja of Cooch Behar, and one of her granddaughters married the Maharaja of Jaipur and became the famed Maharani Gayatri Devi who founded schools for girls in the kingdom.

Down the ages, women have attempted to express themselves through the arts. Depending on the era and location, they may have faced challenges. Mary Cassatt, born in America in the mid-19th century, blazed a trail as an artist during a time when most women of her background were confined to their homes. Some English writers, such as Mary Ann Evans, had to write under a male pen name: George Eliot. Jyotirmoyee Devi Sen is among the earlier women writers of modern Bengal, when most women were not allowed educational opportunities.

In translating the stories, I have delved deeply into the history and culture of that period and have attempted to show what the author intended. Sometimes, in translation, one may need to provide a more detailed description to convey the original meaning.

Bibliography

Craze, Sophia. *Mary Cassatt*. New York: Crescent Books, 1990.

Eisler, Riane. *The Chalice and the Blade*. San Fransisco: Harper & Row, 1987.

'Focus on Buddhist Women's Association,' *Buddhist Temple of San Diego*, https://www.buddhisttemplesandiego.org/bwa-background-history (accessed on 19 May 2022).

Ghose, Indrani. 'Reigning Queens,' *Deccan Herald*, https://www.deccanherald.com/sunday-herald/sunday-herald-articulations/reigning-queens-808885.html (accessed on 19 May 2022).

Gimbutas, Marija. *The Language of the Goddess*. San Francisco: Harper & Row, 1989.

'Hetaera, a Female Companion, and Advisor in Ancient Greece,' *The Role of Women in the Art of Ancient Greece*, http://www.rwaag.org/hetaera-3 (accessed on 19 May 2022).

Lewis, Bertha H. *Beautiful Masterpieces and their Stories*. Atlanta: Whitman Publishing, 1936.

Mitra, Debala. *World Heritage Series: Sanchi*. Archaeological Survey of India, Government of India, 2003.

Nath, Aman. *Jaipur: The Last Destination*. Mumbai: India Book House, 2005.

Rawlinson, H.G. *India: A Short Cultural History*. 1937. New York: Frederick Praeger, 1965.

Sen, Jyotirmoyee Devi. *Raja Ranir Joog* (Bengali). Akla Printing Press, 1980.

'Studies in the Bengal Renaissance.' Third Edition. National Council of Education Bengal, 2002.

Tsultrim, Allione. *Women of Wisdom*. New York: Snow Lion Publications, 2000.

Whiton, Augustus Sherrill. *Interior Design and Decoration*. Fourth Edition. Harper Collins, 1974.

Wikipedia contributors, 'Maitreyi,' *Wikipedia, The Free Encyclopedia*, https://en.wikipedia.org/w/index.php?title=Maitreyi&oldid=1077838740 (accessed May 19, 2022).

BENEATH THE ARAVALLI HILLS
Dhapi

Unfolding a map of old Rajputana, one would see rivers and mountains crisscrossed by spidery railway lines; in a village that nestled against a hillock, a little girl was born.

The names of her three sisters had been chosen with care by her family: the eldest, Mohur, after a gold sovereign; the second, Kesar, which meant "saffron"; and the next, Kasturi, for "fragrance." When their youngest arrived, the parents named her Dhapi or "Enough".

Beneath the Aravalli hills, the fields of barley, millet, wheat and ripening corn spread out like squares on a verdant and tawny dhurrie carpet. Tracts of land, too sandy for cultivation, were left fallow and windblown mounds of earth dotted the landscape; the village itself was small, consisting of a mere cluster of thatched mud-brick homes. The farmers, hairdressers, priests, businessmen and Kshatriyas, or those of Rajput descent, lived in distant harmony within the rigid caste hierarchy adhered to so strictly out in the country. Daily, the villagers congregated by the well; the men stood to one side, exchanging news and smoking hand-rolled tobacco, and the women, balancing an array of pots stacked pyramid-fashion on their heads, conversed with friends.

The farm women's gazes were steady, smiles serene, stature petite and complexions coffee-brushed with russet. The Rajput women, on the other hand, were of striking height with aquiline features, flashing eyes and pale skins. Warriors and nobility had their wives, but they also culled their concubines from among the village girls; over the course of centuries, the descendants of such unions became a caste unto themselves known as Darogas. It was in such a household that little Dhapi was born. The beauty of their great-grandmother, who had stolen the heart of a nobleman, as well as the good looks of their paternal ancestor, found full flower in all the girls, but in the youngest it was the most pronounced. No one in the village could rival her in looks.

The parents, in spite of having named her "Enough," took as much care over her appearance as they did her sisters. The mother braided her youngest daughter's hair with red ribbons and regularly placed a fresh *bindi,* a dot the size of a coin, on the child's forehead; a thin silver necklace, leaf-shaped earrings, bangles and anklets completed the girl's attire.

In a steady rhythm, the swollen goatskin bag rose from the well and tipped over, flooding the furrows while the farmers guided their oxen as the beasts tugged at the ropes attached to the vessel of water. From time to time, village girls dipped their hands in the gullies and giggled as the cool liquid flowed through their fingers; with cheerful insouciance they stacked the filled pitchers on their heads and strolled homeward.

Women young and old, all carrying pots, marched daily up to the well and stood in a queue, keeping a careful distance from the men. Dhapi's three older sisters were no exception; armed with containers fashioned from a blend of clay and ground metal, they came with the youngest more often than not in tow. The air reverberated with peals of feminine laughter and the sloshing of water as the women scrubbed their vessels till they shone.

One morning, the near-idyllic atmosphere vanished. As the women and girls approached the well, they drew their long scarves across their faces in silence. Clutching their veils but maneuvering open a tiny aperture near one eye with their little finger, they gazed at the scene before them. Beneath the spreading fig tree stood three men in crimson tunics, narrow trousers and creased pastel turbans; gleaming metal diskettes dangled from their fingers. Some distance away, two women, both in their early middle years, leaned against a tree. Attired in muslins and silks, veiled in scarves edged with gold threading and with silver necklaces and bangles that glittered, they moved towards the group of silent women.

The villagers returned no overtures and remained immobile. The little boys and girls drank in the details of dress and manner of the newcomers and sped homeward; within minutes, the entire town had learned of these exotic arrivals.

The retinue of crimson-clad guards sporting ceremonial swords and trumpets had accompanied the female visitors and an occasional blast rent the still air. Impelled by a deep curiosity, more women gathered and among the crowd, Dhapi and her sisters pressed forward; in her dull green skirt, a yellow blouse of coarse cloth with white polka dots, her scarf slipping off her head, the child gazed enthralled at the strangers.

Word spread of the newcomers' stunning jewelry, the silken sheen of their clothing and their charming manner of speech; to the surprise of the local folk, these visitors returned every day.

Each morning the ladies of the village hastened up to the well. They absorbed details of the sumptuous apartments and of the queens whose limbs were covered in gold; the lives of the concubines and the king's many loves added an unusual zest to the stories which they only partly understood, but in a bemused manner begged for more. They heard about palaces so large that it took a person more than a day to walk the entire length and breadth of their walls, of fortresses where there was a city within a city, of the capital of their kingdom where roads were paved and the rows of street lamps lit at dusk by lamplighters.

"You mean they don't have dirt roads or cart tracks like we have here?" a woman said.

"Dirt roads?" The speaker gave a sniff. "What's more, there are horse-drawn carriages, oxen-drawn conveyances as well as palanquins borne on the shoulders of strong men; you might even be able to catch a glimpse of a bright veil as the men run past.

"As for clothes, the women, though living in *purdah,* dress in such vivid colors, not like the drab garments you wear in these parts. They also own the most exquisite jewelry that you have ever seen."

"You mean to say that there are stores where you can get everything you want? You don't have to wait for market day?" a listener asked.

"Market day? Why, there are shops where things are arranged and stacked for you to choose from. Jewelry stores, fruit and vegetable stands, grain vendors and oh, the variety of pretty, hand-printed cloth you can buy from fabric stalls!"

A woman with graying hair pulled back in a tight knot stepped closer. "Do men do any farm work in the city?"

The visitor shook with silent laughter, her dangling earrings quivered and she raised a penciled eyebrow. "Goodness, farming? There are men who work in law courts as judges and barristers, there are countless big and small businessmen, not to speak of the royal government officials who run the kingdom.

"There in the big city, you will see so many different kinds of people—foreigners too. You might at times catch a glimpse of a man with alabaster skin and eyes like blue or grey stones. Some carriages in the kingdom's capital operate without the help of animals; they travel like the wind all by themselves. Trains stop at the big terminus regularly. There are theaters where people do not act on a stage, but where pictures of humans are shown on a large screen. You need to buy tickets for those, of course."

"What do women do over there?" asked a bystander.

The narrator curled her lips. "They most certainly don't spend their days drawing water from the well and grinding corn. You can buy flour in shops and hire men to bring in buckets. Women just sit at home."

"Just sit at home and do nothing?"

"Well, if they wish they can sing songs, munch on *paan,* those nice piquant betel leaf wraps, and recline on their divans. They don't do anything; they don't have to."

She paused and allowed the distant mirage of luxurious living sink in the minds of the listeners. "Sometimes they may attend a theater or go for a ride, always in curtained carriages, of course."

The teller of tales had woven a spell among the villagers; at day's end, the women would return home and regale their children with edited versions of the stories, at the close of which they would give a deep sigh and say, "But of course, we folks will never see those fabled palaces."

The children, especially the young girls, found these anecdotes more fascinating than any Arabian Nights tales and begged for more. Sometimes, the youngsters slipped along to the well and hovered on the fringes of the crowd.

The visitors from the city, whenever they found such youthful presence nearby, drew them aside and described the dreamlike quality of life at the royal residences. "There are so many beauties in the palace. Some of them even attract His Highness's attention."

"Then what happens?"

The narrator would drop an eyelid. "Why, the queens begin to fear them. These girls become the maharaja's favorites—they are covered with jewels just like the ranis, and one or two of them may enjoy more power than the chief eunuch. What is more, an especially favorite concubine may wear gold anklets presented by the king."

Mesmerized, the audience distilled the information and allowed it to seep into their young brains.

"Golden anklets? It is wrong to wear gold on your feet," Manphuli, the village goldsmith's daughter, said. "Why, the Patel-ji family is very rich, but even his daughters don't wear those. You must never wear gold on your feet."

The visitor tittered. "Rich family, Patel-ji! It is wrong to wear gold on your nether limbs! Come with me and I predict that at least one amongst you will wear golden anklets. The king himself awards the title Tazimi and presents the ornaments. We have filled the harem with so many pretty girls. Why, look at Sarvati Bai, she came as a young *patri*, advanced to *pardayet* and then on to *pashowan* before our very eyes. Didn't she receive the award? The king and the queens partly rise when she approaches them. She has two sons by the king and a villa on the palace grounds. She also has her private palanquin, just a village girl like you. Didn't fortune smile on her?"

Manphuli, Ghishi, Dhapi, Kesar and Kaveri stared open-mouthed as dizzying dreams of royal stardom whirled in their heads.

The speaker smiled and her tone was mellifluous. "If you want to visit the city, I will take you with me."

Hope, longing, fear and curiosity flashed in quick succession over the girls' faces, and they gazed at the speaker in silence. Would their parents allow them?

"When can we come back if we do get to go?" asked a young maiden.

Ribald laughter greeted her question. "Why would you ever want to return? You will live like queens, you will have luxurious apartments, the king will visit you, your sons will be titled Lalji Saheb, your daughters Baiji Lal. Why on earth would you want to come back to these windswept wastes?"

Heads bent, Kesar and Kaveri stood ruminating by the well, drawing circles with their toes in the moist dirt. They were somewhat older than the others and lived with their own parents, but were married to men they scarcely knew; nonetheless, they were curious about royalty just like any of the other girls, though were less swayed by stories of palatial splendor. The city dweller cast a careless glance at the teenagers. Her quick eyes noted the silver jewelry affixed to their heads.

She nodded towards them. "I will not take those two; they are already married as I can see. We only look for beautiful, unmarried girls."

She smiled at Dhapi, Manphuli and Ghishi. "We have no interest in those who are married."

The three maidens gazed in rapt attention at the speaker, marveling at the dreamy vista spread before them. Disappointment spread across the faces of the older teens as they relinquished fantasies of visits to the fabled city and theaters and motor car rides.

One morning, the village awoke to the news that Dhapi and Manphuli had vanished. The day wore on and the residents learned that the fathers of those two girls had disappeared too, during the predawn hours. The villagers, typically loquacious, remained wordless. Dhapi's mother clutched at her daughters and stared unseeingly out of the window, each succeeding day. The older girls, Kesar and Mohur, ground the wheat, kneaded the dough and prepared chapatis for the family. At the end of the day, the sisters washed up, but their mother's plate remained untouched.

A week later, the two men returned from the city. Swaggering into the village after their jaunt, they waxed eloquent about the glamor of the kingdom's capital and the dazzling future that lay ahead for their daughters. Crawling with curiosity, the village folk crowded around them, distaste and jealousy on their faces.

"They gave me two hundred rupees for Dhapi."

"For Manphuli, I received a hundred."

A voice was heard in the crowd. "You mean to say that you sold your daughters?"

Manphuli's father fixed a glare on the speaker. After two nights on the town where he had imbibed alcohol that he seldom drank, he was truculent. "Sell my daughter? Did I not raise her all these years? It costs money to feed and clothe children. Why should His Highness get her for free?"

Dhapi's father beamed with pride. "There are so many girls in our little town. They only chose ours. Why didn't they take anyone else?"

Their logic was unanswerable, and one by one, the audience melted away.

The sun dipped behind the rim of the Aravalli range in a flood of crimson and gold. In the distance, a train puffed past the station in the nearby town and its haunting whistle reverberated across the hills; as it vanished from sight, a deep silence enveloped the countryside. The train never stopped at the hamlet, yet with its smoke staining the mauve blush of the firmament, the minds of the older women flew to the girls forever parted from their home. The youngsters would live in undreamed-of luxury, they guessed, but with a pang, the women recalled their shy smiles and easy laughter.

In her tiny home, as the days went by, Dhapi's mother set her daughter's plate out at mealtimes and at night, she stared with a vacant eye at her child's empty corner where her bedroll lay. Likewise, Manphuli's mother spent her days in numb anguish, waiting by the window for the girl she would never see again.

One evening after an ample dinner, Dhapi's father finished chewing tobacco and looked at his wife. "Our daughter is now a *patri*." He paused and gave his moustache a twirl. "They are called *patri*s when they are quite young."

"Once she has learned how to sing and dance, perhaps she might catch the eye of the king. At that time, she will become a *pardayet*. With any luck, our daughter might even attain the rank of *pashowan*, just below that of a queen." He spread out the fingers on his right hand as though counting the years to the dazzling day. "Sarvati Bai from our very own village is a *pashowan* and her new name is Prem Rai."

Tears rolled down his wife's cheeks as she looked at her husband; she had no desire of royal stardom for her daughter, and ever present in her mind were her child's dimples and easy smile.

Almost a decade went by. Dhapi had entered the palace as a young girl, and as all newcomers, she dressed in a tunic and pants of simple cotton. Thin as a child, she was developing into a voluptuous young woman, and her homespun clothing could not hide her breathtaking looks.

Khushanjarji, the chief royal eunuch, felt a deep alarm as he eyed Dhapi. He took an avuncular interest in all the inhabitants and he was fond of the girl: her calm face and childlike prattle amused him, although he knew the ways of the palace. She had not gone unnoticed by the senior concubines and in some kohl-rimmed eyes could be discerned both hatred and fear.

The harem was huge—maids, seamstresses, masseuses, beauticians, dancers, singers, ladies-in-waiting and concubines, but only three queens lived within its walls. The maharani and the ranis enjoyed their own well-appointed villas and the ministrations of their maids and attendants numbering in the hundreds, some of whom had been brought over as part of their dowries, while others had been presented to them by their in-laws.

In this vast menagerie of women, only two men were allowed entry—the king and the chief eunuch. Only during certain festivities were some young men invited and these were the two sons of Prem Rai, the king's favorite concubine. Titled Lalji Saheb, they could enter with the express permission of the eunuch, and then only to observe the dancers from a safe distance. The king always sat on a gold-encrusted chair, with his queens to one side and his favored concubines to the other. After any evening of royal revelry, the entire harem was awash in merry chatter and salacious speculation.

Dhapi, sequestered in the dimly lit corridors of the harem, became consumed with curiosity.

One such night of festivities arrived, this time held at Prem Rai's villa. The king, his queens and concubines sat at one end of the hall, while, one by one, the women guests approached to greet them with the customary *nazar,* a gift of a coin of the realm. Swaying to the subtle beat of the hand drum, troupes of dancers performed to the strains of music in the background. A silver tray containing a flagon of wine, tiny glasses and a plate piled high with gold foil-wrapped *paan,* garnished with whole cloves and cardamom, lay on a silver table. The libation was first offered to the king and then the tray made its rounds among his queens and courtesans. The royal women never touched the alcohol, but merely gestured acceptance. Munching on his golden betel leaf wraps, the king sipped his wine, all the while eyeing the dancers.

Prem Rai watched the performance, but a frown appeared on her brow and her eyes widened as she looked at the center of her twirling troupe. She rose and, professing indisposition, bowed before the maharani and begged leave to return to her rooms.

Startled, the performers stilled their sinuous movements to follow their mistress's swiftly moving form out of the royal arena. At the doorway, the chief eunuch stepped forward and the women gathered behind him and pulled their long scarves over their heads.

The lanterns flickered with a thousand flames and for a fleeting moment, the light shone on a face with a golden complexion and gazelle eyes framed by a mass of ebony hair. The king drew in his breath, but the vision vanished.

Back in her apartment, Prem Rai called out, "Godaveri Bai."

Dhapi came forward and bowed before her mistress while the other girls hovered in the background. In the harem, she always answered to that name, as her birth name had been discarded by the palace ladies as too rustic.

Prem Rai's nostrils quivered. "How many times have I told you not to slip into the dance hall when we have a performance for His Highness?" Her delicate features were distorted with rage; an unbecoming flush mottled her translucent skin. "I do not want the maharaja to see you." She paused and smiled. "Yes, no one need ever see you again." She turned to her personal maid. "Throw her in the rooms below."

All the young women froze. Nobody had ever been banished there in their collective memory.

The dapper figure of Khushanjarji appeared at the doorway. A startled "Throw whom?" escaped from his lips. He collected himself and bowed before the concubine.

"His Highness sends you his regards and awaits your return."

The courtesan's face remained grim, but mollified by the obsequiousness of the eunuch, she followed him back to the assembly.

The moat surrounding the fortified palace ran deep. Water had accumulated over the centuries; during the monsoons the waters rose, threatening to flood the lower regions of the structure, although that danger evaporated as the weather warmed. During the winter months, however, the moat was calm as the fort slanted its reflection on the still surface.

Dark, scaly bodies swam to and fro. In a downpour, the crocodiles, snapping their jaws, came close to the walls, but during the summers, as the water level receded, they basked in the mud on the narrow banks.

Some of the apartments downstairs were sumptuous, others less so, but all were used by the concubines, favored or otherwise, as a summer retreat. A few rooms, several stories below, had a sinister purpose. They were harem prisons. A hapless beauty who had fallen afoul of the favored concubines or whose voice rivaled that of a nightingale's, were more often than not, incarcerated in these cells.

Dhapi, her head bent down, followed the maid who took the girl's hand in hers and walked towards the exit. A wave of fear swept over the young women gathered in corners, yet not one of them dared utter a word of commiseration, and like frightened, richly plumed birds, they fluttered to their rooms. Through the deserted passageways trudged the teenager, clutching the hand of the older woman till they came to the top of a steep stairway. Down the steps they labored, the oil lamp flickering in the servant's hand, until the girl's feet felt leaden and she almost wept with fatigue. When they reached the bottom, the maid drew her charge inside one of the rooms and seated her on the mat in the corner; a worn blanket lay on the floor. "Someone will bring you a lamp and some food later on," she said.

The air was stale and dank and Dhapi shuddered; she opened her mouth, but could utter no words.

The woman glanced at the girl's tear-stained cheeks. "Don't be afraid, I will try to come again." The door clanged shut and she went up the stairs.

The prisoner stretched herself out on the mat and, drawing the thin blanket over herself, drifted into a dreamless sleep. Awakened by a sudden noise, she saw that someone had left two chapatis on an earthenware plate along with a pitcher of water. A small oil lamp stood beside the food. Gazing up at the high window, she saw nothing but blackness outside. Alone in this vast warren of rooms, she shivered. Was that a stealthy footstep in the corridor?

Old tales of terror whirled in her brain: secret murders, sudden, unexplained deaths—these very walls, no doubt, had borne witness to the most malevolent forms of treachery. Icy tentacles of fear enmeshed her and she opened her mouth to scream, but no cry emerged. A soft, swishing sound came to her ears and she clutched at her blanket, her teeth chattering. After that, there was dead silence for a long time. She took a sip of water but could not swallow the bread. She pushed the lamp aside and, sitting with her back to the stone wall, stared at the shadows in the room. She wanted to cry out, but her throat was dry; water from the moat lapped against the walls and in her mind's eye, she envisioned saw-toothed creatures slithering past her room.

The following morning, the maid arrived with a plateful of fresh chapatis. She was astonished at Dhapi's wraithlike appearance. "Why haven't you eaten anything?"

Hearing these words, the prisoner clung to the woman's knees. "Please let me go home. I want to go back to my mother,

Burraranji. I will never again enter the festival hall. I don't want to come back here."

"If I let you slip away, I am sure to be beheaded. Am I not human? It is cruel to imprison you in this clammy cell. Why don't you try to eat something, and let me see if I can arrange for a pardon. Please don't starve yourself."

When the woman left, the girl shook with silent sobs while the bread lay untouched and hardened. She longed for her mother, her sisters, their small family farm and the sedate pace of village life. Nights and days blurred into a meaningless mass for her; at times, she nibbled her food, but she could scarcely swallow a morsel. The room grew colder and, seized by night terrors, she shivered as she slept.

Weeks went by, until one evening the chief eunuch and the maid arrived at the prison. They unlocked the door, the flame of the oil lamp flickering in the stagnant air, and stared aghast at the skeletal appearance of the teenager as she lay in a fitful sleep, plagued by a hacking cough.

"Bai, Godaveri Bai," the eunuch said.

Dhapi opened her eyes. "Sir?"

"Will you come with me? I have received orders to bring you back."

Her eyes closed, but a faint smile appeared on the young woman's lips.

"Thank Khushanjarji, give him a salaam," the maid said.

The captive lay inert.

The guardian of the harem turned towards the stairs. "I will release her tomorrow."

At daybreak, the iron door at the top of the stairs groaned open. The eunuch held the lantern aloft and his two companions climbed down. When the maid unlatched the second door, Manphuli ran across the room. Anxious about the fate of her childhood playmate, she had begged to be allowed to accompany them.

The room was dark and she knelt down by the girl and grabbed her arm. "Wake up, we have come to take you back with us."

The light from the eunuch's lamp fell on the bed in the corner. The pitcher of water had tipped over, sending a tiny rivulet towards the door.

With dawning horror, Manphuli looked at Dhapi's eyes staring sightlessly at the ceiling.

Frame-Up
Maji Saheb

Maji Saheb Rathorji awoke and sat up, her pupils dilated and breathing shallow; it had been a disturbing dream. In the dim glow of the silver lamp, she saw her ladies-in-waiting fast asleep beyond the foot of her bedstead, and in the adjoining room, she discerned the recumbent figures of the maids. The apartment was soundless except for the sibilant breathing of the women. A sliver of moon rose in the indigo sky and a light breeze blew in the fragrance of night-blooming jasmine from the rooftop garden. The maharani sat motionless and tried to call out to an attendant, but could utter no words. This was a recurring phenomenon; she recalled that fateful day many years ago—she had been twenty at that time.

Early in the evening she had given birth to her only child, Ram Singh. Fatherless, he was both heir and ruler. The delighted priests showered blessings on the infant and chanted countless mantras and prayers. The ministers of state heaved a sigh of relief and delivered greetings to the newborn, and the ladies of the palace arrived in droves to welcome the boy to the world. The housekeeper of the harem, wreathed in smiles, hastened to congratulate the mother and baby. The entire kingdom was engulfed in a tidal wave of joy.

She barely remembered the exuberant tumult that had swept through the nation, but recalled the overwhelming relief that had coursed through her limbs. Doubtless she had been happy, but would it have mattered if she had had a daughter? A faint smile appeared on her lips. The prime minister and his aides would have encouraged her to adopt a lad from a distant branch of the royal family no doubt, and as a painted puppet, she would have been forced to acquiesce to their demands.

Tired after a long labor, she had fallen into a deep sleep, but as she stirred she sensed that someone was standing by the bed. Through half-closed lids she saw a man looking down at the baby. This person was no stranger, but her husband, dead all of six months. He was clothed in the same outfit that he had worn during the Holi festival when the palace had been awash in color.

A fearsome image had appeared in her sleep-befuddled brain that night, following the revelries: her spouse in a crimson tunic caked with blood lying beside her, his body cold to the touch, the eyes staring into eternity and face tinged blue. She screamed and then fainted. She could not recall how long she had remained unconscious, but regaining awareness, she found herself alone in bed, surrounded by palace functionaries.

The housekeeper stood nearby, murmured a few soothing platitudes and whispered in a quick aside to the maids. Shortly afterwards the chief eunuch, Dilkhush Khan, arrived. The queen looked at the man with, wide, frightened eyes, fearing the worst, and demanded to learn the whereabouts of her husband.

He reassured her, "His Majesty is down with a raging fever. Your Majesty passed out, so we moved you to another room. He is resting. Have no fear, the doctor is attending to him, our priests are preparing an elaborate ceremony and invocations to the deities are being made over the sacred fire. Wheat, millet and other grains are being distributed freely to Brahmins, as well as the poor and hungry, in hopes that prayers for his recovery will be answered."

The queen stared at the messenger in disbelief. She could have sworn that it was her husband's corpse she had seen—he had been cold to the touch. Or had it been a mere nightmare? The previous evening she had stayed up late with her spouse, watching the twirling dancers, sipping wine and nibbling on betel leaf wraps. He had been the picture of health. What sudden malady could have afflicted him?

"I want to go and see him now. Send word right away," the maharani said.

Hearing the lady's request, the housekeeper spun around and directed a warning glance at the eunuch. Their eyes locked. The monarch's wife at that time did not quite fathom its meaning, but now wondered if there had been an unspoken message between them.

"Certainly, Your Majesty. Why don't you rest awhile and recover from your collapse before venturing forth? I will let them know that you will be coming. I will be back soon," the male aide said.

Minutes ticked by, then an hour passed, but there was still no sign of the man. The queen kept vigil for his return in an agony of apprehension. She asked the maids to get further news. Word filtered back in dribbles. "His Majesty is unconscious, but still breathing." "His fever has risen." "The doctors are not permitting anyone to see him." "'These are indeed dire times, the astrologer said." "Please do not distress yourself, he will soon recover." "All the ministers have advised complete seclusion."

Another day passed. The maharani, exhausted after a long night, fell into a fitful sleep, but in her dreams heard subdued murmurs indicating that the maharaja was either very ill or unconscious. Early on the third day, Dilkhush Khan informed the stunned queen that the king had passed away the previous night. During the next few days, life unfolded in a nightmarish sequence: cremation, funeral and ritual display of grief. The royal bride, removed from her own family, surrounded by courtiers in the vast palace, yet utterly alone, grieved in solitude.

The decease of the young ruler plunged the kingdom into deep mourning. Whispers arose that all was not right and a dank, heavy pall of suspicion enveloped the kingdom. Word eventually arrived that the sovereign had indeed been murdered. The widow fell seriously ill amidst murmurs surrounding those nearest to the throne.

Six months later, her son was born. Awakening that night after an exhausted sleep, she saw her husband standing in the same outfit, spattered with color, he had worn the day of Holi. She closed her eyes and screamed. The lantern had gone out, and the room was in darkness. At the cry, the maids hurried over to their mistress while one of them quickly re-lit the lamp. The queen sat up and looked at the space by the head of the bed. It was empty. The attendants, concerned for the health of the new mother, plied her with solicitous queries. "Are you in pain, Your Majesty?" "Are you not feeling well?" and so on. She stared in mute wonder at her ladies, unable to ask them the one question that hammered in her brain. Surely, they too must have seen the apparition; why, he was standing right there by the bed.

Days flew by, but when night-time came, insomnia plagued her and so did a lurking fear.

The next Holi festival fell on a full moon night. The queen's rooftop garden was flooded in silver, and the glow slanted into her room. She could not sleep and walked between the flower pots with thoughts of the deceased monarch whirling in her mind. This time last year she could have sworn that her lifeless lover had lain beside her, but the body had vanished. She returned to bed and fell into a dreamless sleep, but awoke a few hours later to find the visitant in the same red shirt standing by the bedpost, his face an odd shade of blue.

Time passed; she had been without a consort for twenty years and a mother for almost as long. During her long widowhood, she had retreated into a jewel-studded shell, emotionless and unapproachable. Now, after so many years, why did that dreadful phantasm appear?

Searching her mind, she recalled an incident that had occurred a few days ago. The wife of a palace sweeper, half-crazed with grief, had sought audience with the maharani. The supplicant's husband was due to be hanged, and could Her Majesty save him? The queen learned the story from her ladies-in-waiting. The man had had two companions, the younger being this woman. The housewives had quarreled and upon the instigation of his beloved youthful spouse, he had beaten his first partner with such severity, that she succumbed to her injuries soon after. He was immediately arrested for murder.

"Your Majesty, she has heard that your son has powers of clemency. By the time her appeal makes its way to the maharaja it may be too late. She begs that you intercede," an attendant said.

The queen rose and went to the front veranda and saw the woman who sat weeping on the ground below, her hair awry and arms upraised, as she shrieked her agony to the heavens. Visibly discomfited by this display of anguish, the august lady retreated into her silken sanctuary. She was restless the next few days. She had barely known the erstwhile ruler. The marriage had been arranged, the wedding conducted in full royal regalia, but the couple had had little time to get acquainted.

His sudden death had stunned her, but had she been grief-stricken like this person? She was surrounded by maids and ladies-in-waiting, yet none was her friend, and as for the female workers, she had no contact with them and knew little of their lives. Many of the dancers in the palace had blossomed into winsome damsels…had the king still been alive, these women would have vied for the position of being his paramour. No doubt, he would have enjoyed the company of a plethora of beauties as his concubines; they had no family, known no other life, nor experienced any deep joys and sorrows, and to flatter and please their maharaja would have been their ardent desire. Her husband would have married princesses from various neighboring kingdoms for alliances must be maintained, but she, as first wife, would have been maharani, the principal queen. If there had been rivals for his affection, perhaps she, too, would have been wracked with jealousy like this pitiful wretch; if there had been time for tenderness, she would have understood the grief.

She shivered in the dark, staring out of the window. She sat for a long time on her bed until the eastern sky above the Aravalli hills turned crimson when the queen breathed a silent prayer.

She rose and, after taking a bath, dressed in freshly laid out finery, she entered the puja room to say her prayers, then sat in meditation for a long time. She felt utterly alone, and of late, sensed her own isolation with a sharp keenness. Living in sumptuous splendor, she was surrounded by attendants, but no friends; life in a gilded cage had its pleasures, but the stark loneliness was hard to bear.

The nightmares were occurring with alarming frequency. Was there a hidden message? The air had been thick with suspicion when the maharaja died, but no official inquiries conducted. It was astonishing how everything was swiftly cloaked in secrecy and hurried along. Did people suspect her? If only she could talk to her family, but her mother was dead and sisters married to princes elsewhere. For the last twenty years, she had languished as both queen and prisoner. She arrived at the conclusion that royal birth forever condemned one to an icy cell of loneliness. Did her brothers and sisters suspect her of the ultimate calumny? In the Ramayana, Sita herself was falsely accused of disloyalty, but found release in death. She, however, had been suspected of far worse. Was that why the king kept reappearing in her dreams? Was his spirit ever-present in silent condemnation?

A maid came to the door. "The woman has come again and begs an audience with Your Majesty and asks that you come out to the *jharoka*. She cries non-stop and seems unhinged with grief."

The queen rose from her contemplations and stood on the small latticed balcony. If the troubling dream had not occurred the previous night, she might have brushed the petitioner aside.

The agitated lady prostrated herself on the ground. "Oh Maji Saheb, you understand the sorrow of early widowhood. Please have pity on me. You are aware of the heavy burden of murder, but my husband is stricken with remorse. A word from you will save him, I beseech you."

The dowager froze and stared unseeingly straight ahead. She walked back to her meditation chamber in silence. Yes, she knew the loneliness of being bereft of a spouse, or more tellingly, that of being a royal widow. She knew too, the price of assassination and the yoke of false accusation.

Later, she sent word to her son to free the man from the gallows and mete out an alternate punishment.

Legend has it that in the Mahabharata, King Dhrupad's sons played a trick on old Drona by offering him powdered rice dissolved in water instead of the milk he desired, and had been convulsed with paroxysms of mirth at his puzzled face. In the royal harems, through the ages, dancers enacted scenes from the ancient epics consisting of dramas depicting love and longing, hope and despair. The sweet sorrow of the partings of Ram and Sita, Radha and Krishna, Arjun and Subhadra, Madalsa and Ruru, and Savitri and Satyavan, were played out nightly on the marble terraces and pavilions. Sprays of water from the fountains mingled with the tears of the audience at the poignant conclusions. A panorama of romance unfolded, which the queens, ladies-in-waiting and concubines thirstily eyed. They, who had no lovers, lived vicariously through the artistes and, at the conclusion of each performance, their lashes trembled with tears. Exquisitely attired and cocooned in creature comforts, they whiled away their days mesmerized by a mirage of lovelorn lives. As Dhrupad's sons had teased Drona, Fate had played a trick on these women.

One day, scattered thoughts whirled inside the maharani's brain: a recollection of a festive autumnal night during Navaratri when the moon glowed golden in a violet sky. The décor and dress that evening was marked by a near absence of color. The ceremonial gathering was held in the old portion of the fortified palace and against the backdrop of the ancient ramparts, the court glittered. All the ladies wore shimmering silks in the palest of pastels; on their limbs glittered crystal-clear gems and silver, but by custom, not a trace of gold. Between the marble columns, gleaming in the muted light, a luminous palette of subtle pinks and yellows swirled and eddied around the royal newlyweds.

She had been dressed in ivory silk and wreathed in pearls and diamonds set in silver. The king, a youth of eighteen, was younger than she by two years. Moonlight flooded the open terrace, the flickering rooftop lanterns casting a glow on those assembled. Blushing, she rose and greeted her husband with the customary *nazar*, the gift of a gold coin wrapped in a cream linen handkerchief. This was the first time that she saw her spouse up close: tall and with a superb physique that reflected his athletic prowess. Smiling, he accepted her gift. Eyes downcast and face flaming, she slipped into a seat beside him and stole side-long glances from time to time.

The performance began and while the young maharaja sat engrossed by the dances, his wife gazed dreamily into the distance. Words of advice from her own family buzzed in her ears. When the marriage had been arranged, there was no dearth of admonitions. "Yes, you are older than he, but instead of being a princess you will now be queen."

The more astute among the senior ladies-in-waiting remarked, "Don't be satisfied with just being the principal consort, of what use is being maharani, if you cannot be a mother? So what if the king marries again, you can give birth to the next heir to the throne."

Full moon nights came and went and the Vasant Panchami festival, celebrating the first hint of spring, approached; the ladies-in-waiting made veiled allusions, but the bride merely stared at them. As a child, she had heard of the epic romance between Arjun and Subhadra, Prithviraj and Sanjukta, and the love, longing and despair of Radha and Krishna, but she was innocent of any carnal knowledge or passions. The night her husband had spent with her, and the succeeding evenings, he had been ardent enough, but had she really experienced any tumultuous emotions?

The palace was abuzz in eager anticipation when word broke out that the maharani was pregnant. The queen's ladies smiled at each other; they had conspired to bring about this joyful event, and power lay in the womb—as long as the baby was a boy.

The revelries were halted a few weeks later by the sudden death of the young monarch. At the start of the mourning period, the chief eunuch arrived at the door of the maharani's apartment and, making a deep obeisance, requested that all her jewelry be sent to the treasury. So began the pregnant queen's austere journey into royal widowhood. Women whispered amongst themselves that there remained no fear of rivals, and if the child was a son, he would be born not a prince, but king. Overwhelmed with grief, yet over time, the young widow found herself scourged by veiled accusations of regicide.

The dowager emerged from her mental foray into the past.

Two weeks later, the maharaja sent word to his mother that the prisoner faced harsh discipline, but would not be hanged after all.

The sweeper's wife arrived at the gates with not only her own progeny but also her stepchildren, and prostrating herself near the entrance, proclaimed her thanks to the kind lady. "Perhaps, I will never see my husband again. He may remain imprisoned for life, but at least he is still alive. With God's grace he may even be freed sometime in the distant future. If not, at least he is spared." She glanced at the youngsters and her face puckered. "But I will have to bring them up all by myself."

The royal widow listened in silence to the maids as they described the woman's wails of gratitude and shivered at the ferocity of her passion, passion that she had never known or ever will experience. She wondered too, if the minion believed her to be a murderess.

She sank into gloom and returned to her suite while days slid by in a seeming emptiness despite the religious ceremonies and occasional tableaux, and yet, in the deep silences of night, she found no peace. Her son's twenty-first birthday arrived. The palace kitchens were in the midst of preparation for a magnificent feast ordered by the queen mother and indeed, the cooks had been urged to prepare the most delectable confectionery, large portions of which were to be distributed to all the employees and their families in town. That morning, the young monarch made the annual visit to the maharani's villa to receive her blessings. Her eyes widened as they rested upon the youth, he seemed the very image of his dead father.

The visitor perceived that she was thinner than he last remembered. "Are you not well, Mother?" he asked.

She gave a wan smile.

These pleasantries over, they lapsed into an awkward silence. A short while later, the king took his leave.

The consort, still beautiful in her early middle years, appeared to have aged; an incurable malaise seemed to have afflicted her. Widowed at twenty and although shocked at the death of the erstwhile ruler, she had managed to recover, but now, so many years later, she seemed to be burdened with a secret encumbrance. She was innocent, yet the weight of a two-decade-old false accusation gnawed at her. After so much time, whom could she confide in, who would believe her?

Surrounded by women yet completely alone, she sought solace in the sacred scriptures and ancient epics; convinced that no other woman in history was quite as wronged as she was, the queen sank further into a listless stupor. Why, even Sita successfully passed the 'fire test' and was welcomed back into the bosom of her family. Radha had faced heartache, and Tara, Kunti and Ahalya had experienced their shares of sorrow, but no one had been so marooned in a sea of loneliness as she. History would always cast her as the arch villainess, indeed Kaikeyi's machinations paled in comparison to regicide.

The queen fell seriously ill. In a constant stream various functionaries came to minister to her needs. The physician prescribed several potions, the astrologer made prophetic pronouncements after studying the alignments of certain planets and the priest duly made propitious offerings to the deities.

One morning, the doctor arrived and placed his bag on the table.

"Tell me honestly, will I get better?" the patient asked.

Surprised, the greying man stared at the thick velvet curtain hanging between them. "I have not checked your pulse of late. May I have your permission to do so, Your Majesty?"

A thin bloodless wrist stretched out, but remained behind the draperies. At the queen's dismissal conveyed by an attendant he rose and left, casting a curious look behind him.

On another day, the maharani summoned the astrologer, who laid out the lady's planetary charts and in a low monotone began describing the alignment of the benevolent and hostile stars.

"Please let me know quickly, how long do you think I will live?" she said.

A maid peered out from behind the curtain and relayed the question to the visitor sitting on the other side.

Startled, he eyed the opaque screen, perused the documents again and cleared his throat. "These heavenly bodies will remain in this position for another three months. By then the pall that they have cast on Your Majesty will disappear and you will begin to get better. I will say a special prayer so that any celestial malevolence is diminished. There is nothing to fear."

Relieved, the woman gave a faint smile. Upon receiving generous compensation, the man took his leave.

Three months passed and the queen's health took a turn for the better. The multitude of medications prescribed by the doctor, the innumerable prayers by the priest and invocations to the stars by the soothsayer had done their work. The widow, pale and drained of energy, languished in her room. Tormented by a maelstrom of emotions whenever she recalled her late husband, she attempted to envision the lives of ordinary mortals and their families.

Two months went by. The maharani suffered a relapse and fearing that her days were numbered, she sent word to her son. The chief eunuch returned with a message from the sovereign, stating that he would visit that evening. A silver chair, inlaid with gold and layered with silk cushions, was placed beside the queen's bed.

Seated inside a palanquin borne on the shoulders of sturdy servants, the king was carried through the maze of alleys leading to the women's quarters on the royal grounds. He alighted in front of his mother's villa, glittering at every step. Sporting gold anklets, pearl necklace and ear-studs, with diamond clasps on his wrists and clothed in the finest of silks, he came to the entrance. A brocaded turban rested on his head. He took off his embroidered calf-skin shoes before he entered the bedroom.

The invalid glanced at the visitor. "The reason I have called you is to tell you about the night your father died."

The occupant of the throne crinkled his forehead. That his mother was not well, he knew, and had thought that perhaps he was being summoned to her bedside to make bequests to favored courtiers or for a temple construction and special ritual, or donations to places of pilgrimage.

"Tell me about it," he said.

"Do you know anything at all about your father's murder?"

His eyes widened. In his childhood he had heard the palace gossip, learned of the supposed culprits, the suspicions swirling around the queen and even the reasons as to why the accused, when apprehended, had been sentenced so lightly.

The maids lit the little silver lamps and the large lantern in the corner of the room. The light fell on gold-framed pictures of the deities: Radha and Govinda, Vishnu and Lakshmi, Narayana in a state of eternal repose, Rama and Sita in the wilderness of Dandakaranya, and Shiva and Parvati atop Mount Kailash. Another wall was entirely a mural of a holy scene.

The maharani glanced at the divinities. "Please seek their blessings."

The youthful ruler rose and, folding his palms together, bowed before the sacred artwork then sat down with his head bent and avoided his mother's gaze. He had displayed little inclination for marriage. It was whispered that his distaste for nuptials was due to his father's shocking and untimely demise.

The queen gazed at her son, despair written all over her face.

The young man, his face a frozen mask, stared at the floor.

Twenty years had come and gone since that terrible night. In the anguish of the moment, the ministers had demanded that the murderers be brought to justice. Suspects had been found and duly reprimanded. Most of those senior officials were either dead or enfeebled with the passage of years. The boy had learned the names of the criminals as he came of age and the widow too, had been informed at the time.

What a stern, set expression he had, thought the woman; he was not her child, but judge and jury. Gossipmongers had cast aspersions on her character, but with her own end near, she ardently wished that at least her offspring discover the truth. She fixed him with an imploring look and in a barely audible voice began her story.

"All day long we were scattering pink and red powder at each other. Your father joined us on the terrace with a gold squirt gun in his hand. He soaked us with colored water—what a sight we all looked, smeared in crimson and mauve! Later, we bathed and changed into fresh clothes. In the evening the performances began. We heard talented singers and watched the dance dramas. We were awake until the early hours of the morning, munching on betel leaf wraps. We finally went to bed, in fact, I was so exhausted that I fell sound asleep. In the morning I saw your father beside me, dead." The maharani faltered and sat with eyes downcast.

Her son remained silent for a long time. "Did you see anyone nearby? Did you call for help?"

"I screamed and then fainted. After recovering from my swoon, I did not see him again."

"Was he already dead when you first woke up, or was he still breathing? What do you think?"

"My impression was that he was gone."

The maharaja raised his head. "What do you believe? Who killed my dad? At any time over the years, did you hear or sense anything suspicious?

The lady pondered the question. "I cannot really say who might have been responsible. Your father was a mere teenager at that time. But as I recall incidents of those horrible days, I would tend to suspect the harem housekeeper and the chief eunuch."

"Dilkhush Khan? He's dead. And the woman? Why didn't you tell me all these years? Or voice your suspicions then? You could easily have had them charged.

His face grew stern and eyes clouded with mistrust.

The queen directed a tortured gaze at her son. "I did not realize then that they were the culprits. Later, I sensed a coziness between them. Together, they ruled the roost after your father's death. All funds disbursed from the treasury for harem expenses were managed by the eunuch. Who knows what they pocketed? Besides, whom could I tell? If I wanted to send word to anyone, either verbally or by letter, it would all have to go through that man. Once I did question those two. They merely laughed and said, 'Everyone believes that Your Majesty killed the maharaja, because you wanted to reign over the entire palace.'"

"Why did you not inform me of this earlier?"

"When you were five years old, the cabinet ministers requested a meeting with you. After that, they took you away from me. You were raised by tutors, aides and government ministers. From time to time, you were allowed to see me.

But your visits were brief, and we were seldom left alone." The maharani paused and fell into a reverie.

The ruler remained silent.

"Yes, you matured quickly," the woman said, her voice breaking. "Let me tell you about my strange dreams."

In a disjointed fashion, she described the nightmares.

"Where is that housekeeper now?" he asked.

She frowned and closed her eyes. "A year ago, she took leave and went back to her village."

Her eyelids fluttered and she turned towards the youth and flashed a beseeching gaze. The bedside chair was empty.

The attendants gathered around the divan. "When he left, His Majesty asked us to give you more medicine."

The dowager's lower lip quivered. Why had not the king voiced any concerns? How could he vanish without a farewell? Or, did he think that she had fallen asleep? Their relationship, always distant, seemed to have ended on a frigid note. Did he doubt her story? Had he no further questions? She cared little if others knew the truth or not, it was only her son who mattered. No, the world still had no mercy, only condemnation. She took a shuddering breath and her eyes welled with tears.

"Blow out the lamps," she said.

A procession of doctors, priests and astrologers arrived over the next few days with a diet of potions, nostrums and soothing platitudes, knowing that the maharani was at death's door, but eager to help alleviate her distress.

By royal command, messengers were sent in search of the former housekeeper; they went from village to village in quest of the elusive employee. Meanwhile, the queen, visibly weak and stricken with ill health, died.

In the midst of the elaborate funeral, the fugitive was found and brought to court. Heavily veiled, she prostrated herself and, weeping copious tears, professed great sorrow at the demise of the dear Maji Saheb.

"Who killed my father?" asked the sovereign.

The woman's mouth hung open, her lamentations in abeyance.

A tremor appeared in the king's voice. "Can you swear that Her Majesty knew absolutely nothing about the murder? Tell me the truth and after that, leave my presence and never return," he said.

The accomplice stole a fearful glance at the sentries clasping their scimitars. In a halting tongue, she narrated the entire plot and described how they had connived to frame the blameless young widow. She trembled as she stood with her head bent, awaiting the death sentence.

The monarch dismissed the conspirator, but remained deep in thought. He had walked away that evening without acknowledging his mother's innocence. The confession had come too late, she was dead.

The Child Bride
Baijilal

I have been shorthanded for days and have had to do all the chopping, cooking and cleaning, not to mention grinding the various spices, and have worn myself almost to a shadow. People have promised to find me a servant, but the few who have come to work have proved unreliable. My apartment is inside a rambling mansion in the old part of town not far from Gangauri Gate, and from my very window, one can see Hawa Mahal with its many tiers of tiny, lattice-covered balconies. I quite enjoy the view of the hills and the distant Amber Fort, and besides, the rent is most reasonable; my husband has a decent job at one of the royal government offices nearby. There are so many dwellings in this huge haveli that I don't even know most of the residents.

Yesterday, the woman who grinds wheat came over. "Madam, do you need a maid?"

I was chopping vegetables at the time, so I set the *boti* with its curved blade aside and came to the door. "Of course I do. Where is she?"

"If you are ready to engage the person right away, I will go and fetch her, but she is unfamiliar with your style of cooking."

"That is not a problem. She can be trained in what needs to be done."

Minutes ticked by, then an hour passed, but still there was no sign of the messenger. I had almost given up hope when I heard a rustle at the doorway and saw her escorting a girl into my kitchen. The visitor was no more than sixteen and wore a long skirt traditional to the region, but was heavily veiled. In fact, the filmy scarf draped over her head came down to the bosom. What little I could see were her pale hands and feet.

"Here is your maid, Madam."

I stared at the newcomer with serious misgivings. She seemed too young to shoulder the burden of the myriad chores around the house, not to speak of helping me look after my children.

"She appears rather inexperienced. Will she be able to do the work required? Why is she so covered up? There are no men at home at this time of day," I said.

The woman nudged her youthful companion. "You can remove your veil, there are no males here."

The teenager parted her chiffon mask with two fingers, baring one eye, and stared at me. Reassured, she slowly raised it till it hung loose around her face.

I must confess that I gazed at her in amazement. This region abounds in beauties, but I had never come across anyone so attractive. The good looks of some of the queens are legendary and the poise, gait and appearance of the village women striking, but this girl was astonishing to look at. Her complexion was as pale as a *champa* flower and lips a deep pink, through which she gave a shy smile, baring even teeth.

"What are you staring at?" the old woman said.

I composed myself and wiped my hands. "She seems so young and untouched, and her palms are so delicate; she has obviously not worked as a domestic aide before. Will she really be able to do housework?"

"Yes, I can most certainly do what is necessary. Just let me know what you want done."

"Water needs to be brought up from the well downstairs, our pots and dishes must be scrubbed clean, the floors must be swept and mopped, the usual sort of chores, but they must be done my way. For instance, the brass vessels must be polished till they sparkle and water for cooking must be filtered through clean, heavy cloth. We Bengali housewives tend to be a little fussy."

She nodded her head. "I will be able to do everything that you require."

"What is your name?" I said.

"Kesar."

The appellation common enough in Rajasthan was befitting, as her lips and fingertips were as pink as the saffron flower.

The escort took a container of whole wheat from me and headed downstairs. "Teach her everything she needs to know."

Kesar proved to be a quick learner, though I often wondered why this pretty girl had decided to work as a maid. She wore a gold *tikli* on her forehead, the chain anchored to the scalp by strands of hair, and her palms were patterned in a floral motif with henna; clearly, she was married. Thoughts raced through my mind. Where was her husband? Did she have any children?

"Where is your family?" I said one day.

"My parents are dead, and so are my grandparents. Only my great-grandmother is still alive."

The story tumbled out. She lived with this aged relative whose eyesight was failing; the girl herself was already married. Indeed, her wedding had taken place when she was a child of seven. Her husband's family was well-to-do and lived some distance away in the kingdom of Jodhpur. The young man, however, had joined the army in British India and been sent to a distant land; they did not know exactly where. Her parents-in-law were dead, but her husband's stepmother was still living, although no one ever bothered to inquire about Kesar. Only once, while the father-in-law was still alive, did they send someone to fetch the young bride. She was ten years old at that time, and her great-grandmother had demurred, saying that her charge was too young. Married at seven, she hadn't yet gone through the *gauna* ceremony; she was still a virgin. Now sixteen, she had not once heard from her spouse.

Over the next few days, Kesar lost her reserve and became firm friends with my young children. She picked up some Bengali, and as my kids spoke fluent Hindi, I would often hear them conversing with each other.

So beautifully did she sing the folk songs of Rajasthan as she busied herself with household duties that more often than not, my vegetables lay untouched as I listened to her in admiration. It was only when Kesar was indoors with me that she dared to remove her veil, and when it was time to return home at the end of the day, she shrouded herself and flitted away.

"My great-grandmother insists that I follow all *purdah* rules. My face and head must be covered at all times outdoors," she said one day.

"Does she ever leave her apartment?" I said.

"No, Granny is very old and cannot see clearly and is afraid to go out."

Months went by, and the teenaged girl settled down well to our household routines. My children adored Kesar, and my daughter taught her some of our own Bengali songs.

One day, the youngsters ran up to me. "Mother, she is like a sister. Don't let her go away. Teach her our language. Then she can live with us forever."

I laughed. "What if the groom comes to claim his bride?"

Their smiles vanished, and they stared at me, their faces glum.

"Don't worry. I do not want to live with his family. I will always stay with you and be your big sister," Kesar said.

The expression on my son's face brightened, and my daughter smiled and slipped her hand into the older girl's.

One morning, my assistant did not show up. She was punctual as a rule, so I thought that her sole family member had taken a turn for the worse and prayed that all would be well. The day wore on, and still there was no sign of her; I began to feel concerned, and as I had no idea as to where she lived, I sent my son downstairs to get news from the wheat grinder. He was gone for a long while.

He returned at last, his eyes the size of dinner plates. "Mother, the husband has arrived. He is very good-looking and is dressed in a khaki uniform, just like a soldier. And do you know, I also saw the granny sitting on a bed, talking to this man. She is thin and very light-skinned. When Kesar saw me, she quickly disappeared from the room and the flour lady took me aside and whispered that I must never tell a soul that she had worked at our house. If I do, then her in-laws might say nasty things and not take her back. The man has come today to take our helper home with him. She won't be working here anymore." He paused and crinkled his forehead. "Some people were saying that this mansion belongs to the old lady."

Delighted that Kesar's spouse had arrived, nevertheless I felt saddened as I had grown fond of the teen, and the thought of not having her around us depressed me. "That's wonderful news. She is married, so she must go and live with her husband. As to talk of this place belonging to her family, that's utter nonsense. Why then would she work as a maid?"

We never saw the girl again after that, nor did she come to say goodbye. I don't even know when she left and did not dare send my son once more to her home; seeing a Bengali boy, they might get suspicious, since we, as outsiders, would have no reason to have any social intercourse with them. The wheat-pounder had said as much to me, and that on no account must word get around that the young lady had sullied her hands with domestic work.

Charming and talented, the teenager had become almost like a daughter to me and a wonderful sister to my children. In the midst of my daily cooking and sundry chores, I often thought about her and hoped that she was happy, that the in-laws were kind and that she was soon blessed with children. Would she visit her great-grandmother again, and if so, would we ever catch a glimpse of her? When we return to Bengal after my husband retires, we will certainly never have a chance of meeting again.

Over a year and a half went by, and late one evening the flour-maker came upstairs in a state of great agitation. "Madam, Kesar's granny is seriously ill and is asking for you. Please come if you can. Throw a *chaddar* around you and cover your face, and I will take you to her."

It was the age of *purdah* in Rajasthan. Seclusion was carried to extremes I thought, though it was far less prevalent among Bengalis; in deference to local custom I threw a shawl over my head whenever I went to the temple.

I reached for my wrap and stood at the top of the stairs and peppered her with questions. "Does she have no family or friends? Has Kesar been informed? Won't she come over? Why does this lady want to see me? What can I possibly do? I am not a doctor. Why doesn't she call one?"

The messenger laughed. "Do you think Kesar can freely visit her own folk like you Bengalis? The family that she has married into is of high rank. It is a *gharana* household. It is not easy for a bride to leave her in-laws' home for quick visits. The great-grandmother is also of great lineage. She has heard a good deal about you and probably that is why she wants to see you. And as for doctors, she is an old woman. Of what use will they be? There is a physician who stops by from time to time, and he has already been informed."

"Why ask for me? I have never met the woman. The girl worked for us, it is true, and I was fond of her and hope that she is happily married. But why does this lady want to see me?"

My husband, who had just finished his dinner, heard the entire tale from the adjoining room. He came and stood by the doorway. "Why don't you go and visit her just this once? Perhaps there is a reason as to why she is requesting you when she can no doubt call upon any number of her own countrymen. Maybe she wants to borrow money and is uncomfortable about approaching relatives."

"Yes, why don't you go and see her, Mother," my children said.

I smiled at them. They had been so attached to Kesar and missed her. I followed the woman as she led me to the aged relative's apartment. We crossed a courtyard and entered a walled alleyway, went up one set of narrow stairs and onto a verandah. I started panting with exhaustion, and the shawl slipped from my head.

My guide turned around and gave a hiss. "Cover up right now, Madam."

I have no patience for this sort of thing. I am not used to veiling myself as completely as the local ladies, let alone stumbling up the stairs in the dark with my head enveloped in woven wool. The hurricane lamp that dangled from my escort's hand cast an eerie glow in the gathering gloom, and I followed this swinging beacon with growing reluctance. Once again, my wrap left its moorings.

"Please arrange your veil. People might be able to see your face if you don't."

I clicked my tongue in annoyance and shrouded myself. We passed a number of apartments and overheard murmurs of conversation in the many local dialects until we came to a stop in an inner courtyard on an upper floor. It was late March, warm during the day but cool at night. I paused to regain my breath, amazed that after all this exertion we were still in the precincts of the same sprawling mansion that was my family's residence.

My companion led me into one of the rooms facing us. When we entered, I gasped. Could this possibly be the dwelling of my former maid? I had until today never visited a Rajasthani home. The only people we associated with were fellow expatriates, but the sumptuous décor of this place seemed oddly at variance with the normal fortunes of an ordinary working-class family.

A woman lay on a bed covered by a faded silk quilt. Near the window stood an earthenware lamp. By her bedside sat a brass pitcher of water, and in a built-in alcove hung hand-dyed long skirts, blouses and veils. Pictures of the gods and goddesses she worshipped—Radha, Govinda and Gangaji—

were on the wall near the bed. The room was spotless. Who did the cleaning, I wondered? I saw that the lady, draped in a Vrindavani sari of soft cotton in pastel prints, was now sitting up. Beneath a smooth crown of silver hair, her finely chiseled features were apparent through the crushed parchment of skin.

"Please sit down," she said.

My annoyance had given way to curiosity. It seemed as though I had been transported to a fairytale castle where a very old but beautiful woman lay imprisoned in an exquisite room. Her manner, poise and speech breathed centuries of breeding. Why had she sent for me and not called upon her own folk were thoughts that lay trapped in my mind. It was clear that she was not a destitute widow in need of aid and had no desire to borrow money.

The wheat grinder meanwhile, pleading unfinished work, excused herself and left, but informed me that she would return later. I glanced at the great-grandmother and observed that she seemed more pleased than otherwise at this.

I smiled at my hostess. "How is Kesar? Surely she will visit you during your illness? Do you have someone to look after you?"

She laughed. "Do you think that the child's in-laws will allow her to leave at a moment's notice? In our kind of family, teenagers once married do not have much freedom to visit their parents. They are all well, and I have heard that she is happy." She glanced up at the pictures of her gods. "They will watch over me."

I gazed around the room, overwhelmed by its lavishness, and once again wondered as to why this lady had asked to see me. I had left my house in haste, leaving a pile of dishes to be rinsed and washed, not to speak of getting my children ready for bed, and I was anxious to get going.

My escort returned and addressed the matriarch. "May we leave now, Madam?"

"Go right away? But we haven't even discussed the matter yet." The aristocrat leaned towards me. "Will you be so kind as to come back another day?"

I wondered if, due to poor eyesight, she needed help with her correspondence. "Is there any particular task you want me to do for you? If you need someone to write a letter, please let me know. I can send my daughter along one afternoon. She reads and writes Hindi perfectly and will be able to help you."

The fragile beauty glanced at my companion, then turned to me with a flash of entreaty in her eyes. "No, I do not need help with paperwork. You must come again, as I need time to arrange things. Mahadev's mother will bring you over. I am blind in one eye, can only see partially through the other, am also very old and have been ill for some time. Otherwise, I myself would have come to visit you."

So, the grain pounder had a name, "Mahadev's mother"; with growing unease, I tried to fathom what kind of help she craved. Though old and half-blind, the woman was still beautiful, and I could see from where Kesar had inherited her looks. I bowed, folded my palms together in a respectful gesture and took leave. She bade me farewell and murmured blessings.

Next day, my children wanted news of my visit. "Mother, please take us with you to the granny; we want to see her."

"The old woman will not like it. They are strict about observing the rules of seclusion."

"What *purdah*! I slipped over and saw her one day. Of course that was almost two years ago and I was younger then," my boy said.

"I am a girl and so can come with you," my daughter said.

"We'll see."

Three or four days later, the flour maker hurried over to my apartment. "The lady is very ill, please come."

I was preparing dinner and looked at the visitor in dismay; although the octogenarian had all my respect and sympathy, I wondered why she couldn't approach any of her own people. I washed my hands, removed some of the pots from the stove, grabbed my shawl, and turned to leave. My daughter, bubbling with eagerness, demanded to come but was refused.

Darkness had fallen and lamps had not yet been lit in most of the apartments in the mansion. I glimpsed Amber Fort in the horizon, etched against the twilit sky and the battlements of Nahargarh Fort on a remote hilltop; the full moon rose, bathing the white spire of a nearby temple in a misty haze. Tonight my messenger seemed preoccupied and marched ahead, so I drew aside my veil and admired the beauty of the moonlit landscape.

The elderly lady sat up on her bed when we arrived. The room was brightly lit. An earthenware oil lamp stood on a table, the flame glowing from one end of the cotton wick. Wax candles, too, were arranged around the room.

"Sit down, Bai. You are like a daughter to me, so today I am calling you Bai, not Baiji. You have been so kind to my Kesar," she said, then turned to my guide. "Mahadev's mother, why don't you leave and do any odds and ends of work that you might have. If you are needed I will ask for you. But wait, whom can I send? Why don't you just sit outside the door, as I need to discuss some private matters."

My companion left the room.

I sat dumbfounded on a divan, while thoughts raced through my mind. What secret business could this lady have with me that this trusted guide could not be witness to? Fear started gnawing at me, yet what was there to be afraid of from a frail woman in this rabbit-warren of a mansion tenanted by countless people?

The resident walked to the corner of the room. Though bent with age, she was tall and moved with grace despite her years. She opened a wooden chest and pulled out a brass container inlaid with silver and enameled with peacocks and flowers. She did not appear to be prostrated by any maladies as my guide had implied and came over and sat beside me. It was only then that I was able to get a good look and marveled at her beauty, still visible in the delicate lines of her face.

She took out a key and, with trembling hands, unlocked the metal safe and pulled out a cloth bag embroidered with gold threading and laid it on the divan. Next, she brought forth an ivory box, followed by others of carved sandalwood.

I sat in rapt silence and watched her pale hands move back and forth unpacking box after box. First, she opened a long case and drew out a necklace; a stream of pearls shimmered from her fingers, and the locket, a gold medallion with painted enamelwork, winked at me in the flickering light. Earrings set with rubies and pearls emerged from an ivory case. From a wooden container, she drew out a series of objects wrapped in red or blue tissue paper. She undid the small packets and revealed diamond rings, gold earrings, pearl nose rings, ruby-studded *tikli*s or ornaments for the hair, and anklets of silver.

She turned the bag upside down. A handful of coins tumbled out and dazzled my eyes.

I stared dumbstruck at this treasure trove and wondered if I were dreaming an Arabian Nights fantasy.

The old woman laid out the doubloons and began counting them under her breath. There was a total of twenty-one gold pieces; some were flat medallions, others mohurs. From another bag emerged pure sterling; some of them were currency of the realm, inscribed with Jharshahi lettering, and a few from British India.

Like a conjuror transforming worn bags into storehouses of untold wealth, she continued performing her magic until the entire bed was strewn with aureate orbs and discs of silver.

She grabbed my hand and opened her mouth to speak, but her voice broke and eyes swam. "Baiji, I am entrusting you with all this. That is why I asked you over several times, because I wanted to get to know you better. Kesar often mentioned your family in conversation. These belonged to her mother, grandmother, me and all her maternal ancestors. My days on earth are coming to an end. There is no one who can really be trusted, so that is why I am asking you to safeguard them. Some of this money is my life's savings. I have managed to keep this booty well hidden; nobody knows about this wealth."

I tried to draw my hand away. My foremost impulse was to flee from the weight of this enormous responsibility.

The lady gripped my palm till her veins protruded and I winced in pain. "It is apparent that you are astonished at all this wealth. Why don't you stay a while and hear my story? You are a busy housewife, so I cannot keep asking for you again and again. My years are weighing me down, who knows how much longer I will live? Please don't leave just yet.

You are probably under the impression that we are very poor, and that is why I sent my great-granddaughter to work as a maid. That I am in want is true, but that need is not due to lack of food or money. This mansion belongs to me, and the rents received more than cover my expenses. Some of my tenants believe that the man who collects payments from them is my brother, and that he is my protector."

She paused and looked at me, pride and gravity mingled in her voice. "I am Maharaja Ram Singh's granddaughter. My father, Chandan Singh, was the son of His Majesty and his favorite concubine. As you may know, all such royal sons, though not princes, are titled Lalji Saheb, but His Majesty was so fond of my father that he conferred on him the title Raja. Acres upon acres of fertile land along with other property were bestowed on him, and like the princes, he lived in a small villa on the grounds of the Moon Palace. I was born there and spent my childhood in the royal residence. I was the eldest daughter and named Ladli Bai, after our Holy Sree Radha Ladliji Devi; in fact, my grandfather gave me that name. They used to call me Baijilal Ladli Bai. You see, princesses are called Baijiraj, but we are referred to as Baijilal.

There is a wealth of stories I can tell you about growing up in the palace, but don't have the time. My marriage was arranged to a young man of good family. A few days after my wedding, the king died, and so did my father some years later. I had a son, and he had a daughter, but neither he nor his wife lived long. I brought up the little girl to the best of my ability and married her off through people we knew. Unfortunately, my granddaughter died while giving birth to Kesar, and her husband remarried and left the infant with me.

The child's father never bothered to inquire after the baby. Perhaps he felt that he would have to pay expenses or maybe feared that the potential wedding costs would be astronomical. In families like ours, dowries can be substantial, and to arrange a suitable match, an ample sum has to be paid. Meanwhile, his new wife had several children, so Kesar has stepbrothers and stepsisters whom she has never seen. Her dad died a few years ago, and thus I am her nearest relative. This mansion is my inheritance to be held in trust for my son and grandson, but as there is no living male heir, the property may revert to the Crown or be passed on to my father's great-nephews.

Concerned that no one would bother about her as she came of age, I searched long and hard for an eligible bachelor and discovered the family of a Lalji Saheb in Jodhpur who had a son of nineteen. Kesar was then seven."

She looked at me with an air of quiet triumph. "Ever since the child came to live with me I have had to plan for her future. There was some money saved up, plus my jewelry. We have always had enough to eat, but I had to sell a lot of pieces to pay for the girl's wedding and dowry, not to speak of my own medical expenses. This is all that I have left now."

I stared at the iridescent bracelets and rings, at the array of necklaces set with emeralds and rubies and at the ropes of pearls cascading over the bed. "All? It's still a king's ransom."

The lady laughed. "Some of these pieces were presented to me by His Majesty on my wedding day. Some of them were from my father. The gold mohur coins that you see were part of my dowry. The jewelry belonging to Kesar's mother and grandmother are also in this pile—they have all found their way back to her.

"I am housebound and have little knowledge of the world. Unscrupulous men have cheated me of money, tenants have not always paid up, and that is why I trust very few people.

"This is my great-granddaughter's ancestral wealth. If I die, the girl's stepmother or stepbrothers can invade my apartment and take away everything. Or my own great-nephews might descend on my property, and whoever comes first will have a free hand. If I had given them to Kesar when she left with her husband, the in-laws might have tried to grab them at the outset due to her youthful naiveté. If I ask for help from any of my relatives, then what has been safeguarded all these years will become common knowledge."

Her eyes filled with tears and she reached for my hand. "It was not for money that she was sent over to work for you. I am a weak and feeble woman and need to rest during the afternoons. She is a pretty girl and it had come to my ears that some of my male tenants had been eyeing her. News of your family had also reached me. Your husband is an upstanding man who works for our royal government, and you are a good woman with bright, well-mannered children.

"I needed to place Kesar in an environment where she would be safe during the day and protected from unseemly overtures by men, for if there was any whiff of scandal, the husband's family would refuse to accept her as she came of age. I have taught the child at home, but since you are all well-educated, I believed that she would benefit from being with you and your kids."

The matriarch clutched my hand tighter. "Will you keep this jewelry for Kesar? You have been like a mother to her. She used to tell me how much your son and daughter adored her."

My head whirled. Being pleasant to a girl who worked for you and offering her snacks of fruit and sweets was one thing; being a personal banker for the young woman's all worldly wealth was quite another.

She continued clasping my hand. I looked again at Ali Baba's hoard spread on the bed and my spirits quailed; I saw a fragile old woman bereft of family support who had single-handedly raised a teenager and was consumed with concern for her future.

"Let me discuss this matter with my husband. There must, however, be a witness to this transaction. After all, I could die or fall prey to greed. Money can corrupt many souls and it is a great responsibility to be entrusted with so much wealth. Please lock up everything right away. With your permission I will bring him over to meet you tomorrow," I said.

The royal descendant sensed my unease and with trembling hands she placed the items back in their boxes. She once again whispered blessings as I took leave.

The following day I wrote Kesar a letter saying that her great-grandmother was very ill. During the afternoon we visited the aged woman and took an inventory of all the jewelry and coins, the sole witness being the wheat grinder.

"May we call a lawyer to draw up custodial documents?" I said.

"No, if you do, then word might get around. Fasten the boxes with sealing wax, and make two sets of records. Keep one list with yourself and give the other to Mahadev's mother, who will give it to Kesar when the time comes. When the day arrives for you to give the jewels to her, you may also hand over your papers, all in the presence of an attorney if you wish. If, on the other hand, God wills that the girl dies, or she has no surviving children, then please deliver the treasure to my great-nephews or their descendants."

She twisted her lips. "A new era is upon us. Kingdoms are vanishing before our eyes, and rulers are hanging up their crowns. The Lalji Sahebs are now going a-begging, their ancestral properties being taxed away. The maharajas are no more. What do they call them nowadays? 'Rajpramukh'? Can you please tell me what that means, Bai?"

The three of us marveled at the lady's indomitable spirit as she handed over her ancestral wealth with a regal air.

A wave of panic assailed me. "What if we died and my children were unable to locate your great-granddaughter's whereabouts?"

She glanced at the pictures of the deities on her wall. "If that is what God wills, then let it be so."

We walked back to our apartment, both of us deep in thought at the enormity of the task ahead. Next morning, I wrote Kesar a second time, urging a visit to her cherished relative as the lady's health was failing.

When I went and told the woman about my attempt at correspondence, her face brightened and eyes sparkled. Minutes later, she lapsed into gloom.

"It is doubtful that the in-laws will let Kesar come and visit me. You do not know our customs and traditions. Let's see if we even receive a reply," she said.

Each passing day I waited for the postman's knock, but my vigil was in vain. Fearing that my piece had not reached, I sent another by registered post. It was returned unclaimed. Meanwhile, a month and a half went by.

One morning, the flour maker came to my door. "The old lady is very ill, but she is still conscious. The great-nephews have arrived, and many people are crowding into the apartment to see her for the last time."

I, too, went to bid farewell, and a day or two later, she died.

Rumors began spreading about the sprawling property as to who would inherit, if anyone. In the midst of all this uncertainty, Mahadev's mother came to me and learned that my various efforts in contacting Kesar had not borne fruit.

"Send a letter with insufficient postage. Among old families in the villages, people do not approve of a housewife coming to the door for a package or any kind of mail. In aristocratic families, too, I have heard, the norms are the same; in fact, women are kept even more under wraps. Write again and say that her granny has passed away. Someone in their household will no doubt take it to Kesar to obtain the necessary funds for the stamp. Do not mention the loot, otherwise her in-laws will arrive at your doorstep like vultures," she said.

"How long can I hold on to all that treasure? There is no strong-room in my apartment."

"Hush, don't breathe a word to anyone. God will arrange something."

Anxiety overtook me. "Hopefully God will, otherwise I am going to be in a divine dilemma. How can I protect her inheritance if they descend on me in force? My husband is away at his office all day. Or what if an ordinary thief decided to burgle my home? He'd certainly find a tidy haul."

My confidante quivered with suppressed mirth but made no reply.

"Perhaps that is the reason why women are not allowed to own wealth, as they are often unable to keep secure what is rightfully theirs," I said.

To my amazement, the missive with inadequate postage accomplished what my registered letter did not. One morning I saw a tall man, Kesar, and a small boy arrive in a curtained carriage and go straight to the wheat grinder's tiny room in the old mansion. The aristocrat's death had left the disposition of the property in the hands of the courts, and the uncertainty had caused some of the tenants to vacate. We found a small home to rent across the street.

A short while later, Mahadev's mother came over to my house. "My suggestion did the trick." She gave a sly chuckle. "But where can they stay? I have only one room, but if I notify any of her stepfamily, they will suspect that there might be hidden booty. The old lady feared as much."

"Bring them over to my house. I can put them up for a night. They are descended from Rajputs, so our dietary habits may not prove such a bar."

Kesar arrived dressed in an ankle-length crimson skirt, an embroidered blouse and a blue chiffon scarf with which she kept herself securely veiled. She wore gold *hasuli* chokers, a skirt anchored at the top with a jeweled waistband, and bangles all the way up to her elbows that flashed molten fire in the morning sun.

She raised her head covering as she approached me, and I observed the gold *tikli* nestled in the center parting of her hair, the medallion resting on her forehead.

Her tresses were braided with red and gold *zari* ribbons which glinted in the sunlight each time she moved. Her fingers sported ruby rings, and the palms and feet were patterned in henna; she wore three sets of silver anklets. Brocaded, beribboned and bejeweled, she looked ravishing. Custom decrees that a new bride should wear finery when she returns for a first visit to her parents' home, and although the young woman's immediate family was no more, she still saw fit to dress well for a trip to the ancestral dwelling.

My husband and children were waiting beside me to greet her. I told my spouse and son to leave, fearing that their presence might offend, as the girl's in-laws were strict about *purdah* rules.

Kesar came over and hugged me, and it was like old times once again. While the menfolk waited in a separate room, she sat beside me and removed her veil.

"Your granny has left jewelry for you, and we have an inventory of it," I said.

"That is why I have come today. There is no need to look at the list, I know exactly what's in the safe."

"You know what she had?"

"Oh, yes, she showed them to me a few years ago and said that she would leave them with a trusted person until I could claim them."

"Will you be able to take them all?"

"Yes, of course."

"The old lady was afraid that your in-laws may try to snatch them from you."

Kesar laughed, but said nothing.

I glanced at the boy sitting beside her. "Who is he?"

She drew the little fellow close and gave him a hug. "He is my son."

The child looked to be about five or six years of age. She had however, been living with her spouse for no more than two years. I remained silent, but a question lurked in my eye.

The youngster rubbed his head against her shoulder. "This is my *chhoti ma*."

It was then that I understood.

"He is the son of my husband's other wife," Kesar said.

Discomfited, I gazed at them both. Plural matrimonial alliances were not uncommon among certain lineages, but I wondered if the matriarch had known. "Have you any kids of your own as yet?"

Kesar shook her head.

"Did your great-grandmother know about this? She was most particular that only your children inherit all this treasure. Was your husband already married when she arranged yours?"

"No, he was single at that time. But during the nine or ten years before I moved into their home, his family found another bride for him. Neither my granny nor I ever knew of this. But he is indeed my son." She ruffled his hair and gave him another hug. "Who is your mama, Sundar Singh?"

The boy glanced up and laughed. "I have two mothers."

He seemed a charming child.

"Will you really be able to take everything? What if your in-laws try to grab some of it?" I said.

"No, they won't. If God decrees that they have my jewels and money, then so be it. Whatever happens is God's will, isn't that so, Baiji?"

The elderly woman had displayed this streak of fatalism too, I recalled. With mounting concern, I entreated the teen to guard the wealth which her august progenitor had hoarded all these years. She merely smiled and hugged the boy even tighter.

Later that day, we summoned a lawyer and transferred the ancestral jewels to her in his presence. I caught my breath as the rays of the setting sun fell on the gems; set in gold, the rubies glowed and the diamonds dazzled white fire. Her husband later carried the boxes to their bedroom, staggering a little beneath their weight. A couple of days later, we bade them farewell, and my daughter gave Kesar one tearful last hug.

The years went by swiftly enough; my girl got married, my son found a job, my husband retired, and it was time to return to our homeland. The monsoons were coming to a close, and the festival of Jhoolan was upon us. We decided that on our way back to Bengal, we must visit the holy cities of Mathura and Vrindavan; it would be both a holiday and pilgrimage. An elderly couple, both of them devout Vaishnavas, were caretakers of a temple dedicated to Sri Govindji as well as being managers of the guest house for pilgrims. They were known to us, and it was there that we stayed during our trip.

Temples by the score dotted the entire landscape of Vrindavan. As in Benares, there are edifices small and large devoted to Lord Shiva, similarly in this place, there are innumerable shrines to Sri Govindji and Sri Radha Devi. Indeed, one of the kings of Jaipur had built a spectacular house of worship consecrated to Sri Radha Ladliji Devi. We traversed the city from dawn to dusk, visiting sites, greeting fellow travelers before returning to the hostelry footsore and weary. During the afternoons, we heard wandering minstrels in the streets and saw puppeteers performing scenes from Krishna Leela. At day's end, we continued to imbibe all that was holy; performers danced the devotional *arati*, the air thick with incense smoke, pungent yet fragrant, and priests sung hymns in sonorous tones as they tended the sacred fire.

Fellow pilgrims told us tales of the macabre and mysterious that they had heard around town. We learned that at dusk, the Nidhuvan Gardens were deserted by all living beings; indeed, even birds and monkeys steered clear of the grounds. The ubiquitous langurs, with their cinder faces, compact furry bodies and rope-like tails, who clambered on temples and rooftops alike, ceased their chatter and deserted the place *en masse* at nightfall. One man had challenged the powers of darkness and had stayed overnight; the following morning he was found—wild-eyed and raving. Another, undeterred by the skeptic's fate, had ventured there one evening. The next day, his family saw him wandering the streets, sane—but blind. The supernatural and the sacred mingled together and among the pilgrims, there were the devoted dozens and the fearful few.

The monsoons gave way to autumn and our long sojourn came to an end; it was time to go home.

Troubled at the thought of the enormous amount of packing ahead of me, I went downstairs in search of the manager's wife.

"I could use some help," I said.

"There is a young woman who would be most suitable. She lives on the premises and is always ready to do odd jobs," she said.

Delighted to receive help at such short notice, I asked, "Is she a Bengali woman?" A fair number of our compatriots lived in the area.

"No, she is a Hindustani girl. But she does have a smattering of our language, doubtless having picked it up from our guests, the majority of whom are from our part of the world. You speak Hindi too, so communication should not be a problem."

Loaded with gifts, I was attempting to repack for the third time.

The innkeeper's wife went down the hall and called out, "Has Kesar arrived yet?"—"Oh yes, she has."

I spun around, but the name was common enough in this region, so I returned to my packing. There was a rustle of swirling skirt at the door. In the dim light of the hurricane lamp, we both stared at each other.

"You? Over here?" I asked.

"Madam, you have come to Vrindavan?" responded Kesar.

Satisfied that we were acquaintances, the proprietress returned in relief to her housekeeping duties. Kesar took over and, with smooth efficiency, deftly packed the assorted souvenirs and saris and secreted them into nooks and crevices of the overflowing trunks and suitcases.

After the initial shock of surprise, the guesthouse employee busied herself with packing while I stood in silence, a myriad questions milling in my brain. From her clothing, it was impossible to discern if she had been widowed, as women of Rajasthan do not shroud themselves in white upon widowhood like us. Her head was bare of the traditional *tikli*, and it was then that I realized that she had lost her husband. Questions hammered in my brain.

She finished packing and the last box was fastened. "Madam, have you come on a pilgrimage? Are you really leaving today? Had I known that you were here, I would have visited you sooner."

Her wrists were devoid of the mark of marital bliss, the traditional green glass bangles. In fact, gold jewelry was absent from her attire and she wore only a silver necklace and bracelet.

"I will take your luggage downstairs," she said.

"No, no, the phaeton driver will come and carry them. The trunks are too heavy for you. Please don't take them, Kesar."

Unheeding, she took a bulging suitcase and hastened towards the lobby as though fleeing from me. The innkeeper's wife came to my room. "It appears that you two are not strangers."

I had been staring unseeingly out of the window at the gathering dusk and upon hearing her voice, I started. "Yes, we have met before. Many years ago, when we lived in a portion of an old mansion near Hawa Mahal, she worked for us for a bit. She used to stay with her granny." I paused and took a deep breath. "But why isn't she living with her in-laws' extended family? Doesn't she have any children?"

"No, she does not. We ourselves have been living in Vrindavan since my husband's retirement, but a long while back we used to live in Jaipur, and he still visits that city from time to time. His family had known her great-grandmother, Baijilal Ladlibai, a most courageous and spirited woman. She was descended from Maharaja Ram Singh and his favorite courtesan. My father-in-law was a noted lawyer and had helped the old lady over some disputes with tenants. Two years ago, my husband went to Jaipur and saw Kesar at one of the temples there. She recognized him and wanted to speak to him. So, he took her aside and asked if she needed any help."

The speaker stepped inside the room, lowered her voice and pulled the door shut. "Kesar was widowed a few years ago.

Shortly afterwards, her husband's brothers and his second wife sent the young woman on a long visit to her stepmother's home. She would recover from grief better there, they indicated. They also said, 'Leave your jewelry in our family vault. It will be safe here. You will be returning soon enough anyway.' So the sorrowing girl left.

"After that none of the in-laws ever came to take her back, nor did they make any inquiries. Her stepfamily began to get annoyed over the unending visit and, not wishing to be saddled any longer, they threw her out. My husband was visiting Jaipur during the Holi festival, and it was then that he met Kesar at the temple. She had been subsisting on food and fruit from the daily offerings that the priests handed out.

"So, my husband immediately wrote a letter to her in-laws. He received no reply. Then he sent a messenger over to their house in Jodhpur and requested that they take the girl back into their fold. Lamenting the changing times, they responded that they were in no position to care for another, things were hard enough for them as it was. When asked to return the jewels if they were unwilling to give the young woman a home, they affected great surprise and said that they knew nothing about them. Everything in their family vault had been there for generations. It was their word against ours. Unsuccessful in his attempt to wrest back Kesar's wealth, he came back.

"He visited the town again a year later, and discovered that she was indeed in dire straits. She lived in dingy dwellings near the temple, and the people who had known of her great-grandmother's august heritage were very concerned for the girl's safety and begged help from him.

"They said, 'Babuji, please take her with you. She barely gets enough to eat and is in poor health. Let her serve Sri Govindji at the temple in Vrindavan. She is safer there than in a big city. If you do not do so, the young lady will either die or fall into evil hands.' She has been here ever since and devotes herself to various duties. She draws water from the well daily, cleans the altar room, gathers and arranges the incense sticks and twice a day receives *prasad* of fruit and sweets, along with an ample vegetarian meal. For occasional chores for me, I give her a monthly allowance. She is such a good-natured girl, and so meticulous in her work."

I opened the door and looked down the hallway and began to wonder where Kesar had gone, for after taking down one suitcase she never reappeared.

"I have sent her to call a carriage. There is a huge rest stop for phaetons and their drivers and horses right by our hostelry. Let us go down, and when the man arrives, we will send him upstairs so that he can bring down your remaining stuff."

We both descended the narrow stairway. I saw her standing in the alcove below the steps, a hurricane lamp in one hand. In the half-light, her beautiful face appeared drained of all expression.

"Why are you waiting here?" I said.

"Keeping an eye on your things."

She was dressed like a maid, in a faded cotton ankle-length skirt and blouse with a much-scrubbed scarf draped over her bosom and head. An image flooded through my mind: that of Kesar in a silk outfit, radiant with joy and cloaked with jewels, ascending the steps of a carriage on the arm of her husband and waving goodbye.

More than a decade later, she was still good-looking, her beauty more vivid in the drab clothing, but her eyes were dulled with pain and had a stunned look in them.

I put an arm around her. "Why don't you come with me?" Reason had fled. Where could I take her to?

"Madam…," she said. Her voice broke, and tears trembled on her lashes.

I put both my arms around the girl. She gave a shuddering sob and, clinging to each other, we both wept.

She wiped her face. "No, madam, I will remain here at the feet of Sri Govindji. This is my fate."

Once again, I was struck by the deep vein of fatalism which I had once witnessed in the old woman.

The manager came and stood behind his wife. "Where will you go? How can you take her with you to faraway Bengal, when she barely speaks the language there? It is best that she remains here. No man will ever marry her, now that she is a widow. Let the young lady serve Sri Govindji at the temple; the devotees call her *kesar chandan*."

Kesar chandan: the fragrant sandalwood paste blended with saffron to form a smooth orange-tinted mixture to be smeared on the feet and limbs of the deities. I knew only too well that destitute widows were more often than not driven to prostitution, so to be of service at the temple and make concoctions for the gods was no doubt a far better fate.

It was time to leave for the station, so we said goodbye to the couple. I reached out and took both of Kesar's hands in mine as she stood with eyes downcast hiding unshed tears. We climbed into the carriage, the driver cracked his whip, and the horse trotted off. We jostled our way towards our compartment, the porters running ahead of us with our luggage.

The train gathered speed, and I looked at my husband. "Why did the in-laws throw her out? She loved her stepson so much that she would have willingly bestowed the jewels and money on him. She had no near relatives, so all that wealth would have reverted to them anyway."

A sliver of memory pierced my brain: the old woman's frail hands sorting and packing with care the necklaces, rings and bracelets to be held in trust for Kesar.

The Queen and the Concubine
Raja Rani O Kesar

"Everybody heaps blame on us," Nalini's grandmother said. "They say that nowadays children are so restless that they cannot sit still for even a moment. All day long, two girls, each holding one knotted end, keep whirring a rope round and round through which another child jumps till she is flushed and breathless. As for the boys, we hear nothing but the clickety-clack of counters sliding on the wooden surface of carrom boards.

"Our folklore no longer interests you. For medicine, we have always taken dried, crushed leaves from the *kalmegh* tree, but now none of you will swallow anything unless it comes in a glass bottle. Although, I must say that some of you can still create the traditional *alpona* patterns, at times. Come autumn, why not decorate this house for the Lakshmi Puja celebration?

"Anyhow, it's getting dark—you kids should all take a break from your hectic games, pull out some mats, spread yourselves out and hear some tales."

Those engaged in the frenetic activities took a pause and laughed. "All right, why don't you tell us a story?"

Grandma shut her volume of the epic, the Mahabharata, with a snap and took off her glasses. "Once upon a time…"

"Goodness," a grandson said, "another fairy tale."

His older brother nudged him, "Be quiet."

"There was a king and he had four queens," continued the narrator, unperturbed. "His wives were from powerful neighboring kingdoms, and their fathers had bestowed upon them, as part of their dowries, vast sums of money as well as troves of gold, diamonds and pearls befitting Rajput royals. To the ruler of course, this was mere spare change. Each bride also brought with her about a hundred beautiful ladies-in-waiting."

"Did the ranis ever get pocket money?" asked the youngest child in the audience.

"An allowance, my dear? They had their own expense accounts, granted directly to them from the treasury. Royalty lived in great style. They owned motor cars, stables of elephants, fleets of steeds and an army of servants."

"I have never heard of a fairy tale with cars in it."

"Well, your mother and aunts glimpsed gleaming Rolls Royces when they visited the palace recently," Grandma said. "The monarch had his own private polo grounds, too."

"These ladies, however, despite their untold wealth, nursed secret sorrows. Their husband seldom, if ever, visited them. He was taken up with hunting and horseback riding, and his many concubines demanded a lot of his attention.

"The queens found time hanging heavy on their hands. What do you think they did? Spend it squabbling with each other? They did not even have that pleasure, since each rani had her own villa, palanquin, female guards and an enormous retinue of maids and attendants. And who would they quarrel over? Their spouse belonged to no one. None of them had any children, so they could not occupy themselves engaging in petty rivalries either.

"Glittering in rubies, emeralds and other gemstones set in pure gold and swathed in fine silks, they lay languidly against their cushions day by day, at times conversing with their handmaidens, or nibbling sweetmeats and sipping cool drinks made from freshly squeezed limes. Sometimes, a hidden longing could be seen lurking in the depths of their eyes."

"Why were they so sad?" asked a preteen.

"Oh, they did not remain unhappy for long. They were after all, well-educated women unlike us folks. To while away their hours, they held pageants and dance dramas in their own sumptuous villas. To do that, however, they were still required to obtain the express permission of the monarch himself. His Majesty was always invited as their most honored guest, and it was only on these occasions did each consort enjoy the pleasure of her husband's company."

The old lady smoothed her hair, sat back and began her story.

Tales from the ancient Hindu epics were usually enacted; stories from the Ramayana, the celestial romance of Radha and Krishna and the valorous deeds of Dhruva and young Prahlad were very popular. The queens themselves, with the assistance of some of their ladies-in-waiting, choreographed the performances. The artistes were all women of the royal residence; none of them had known any other life. Destitute villagers eagerly sold their better-looking daughters to swell the harem ranks, while others freely deposited them at the castle gates. Each princess bride, as part of her dowry, brought over a multitude of female attendants, and it was from among these girls that dancers were culled.

One day, the maharani wished to host a musical soirée, and at her bidding, the senior-most aide, a corpulent and majestic woman, sought His Majesty's consent from the eunuch. The royal permission duly arrived, and she went around the vast palace precincts to personally invite all the harem inhabitants.

Upon nightfall, the junior queens began arriving in silver palanquins. Their ladies-in-waiting and maids sped in happy anticipation through the dark labyrinthine alleyways where at each turning stood huge oil lamps. These were gigantic, shallow, earthenware or stone containers filled with gallons of the inflammable liquid in which swam hand-made cotton wicks, each as thick as a human finger. The flames flickered and cast a pallid glow. The king's concubines, too, had been invited and there were some in this throng who spoke of phantom spirits seen in recent weeks in these inky corridors.

A stripling of a youth fidgeted with the edge of a large woven mat. "Tell us a ghost story, instead."

"I don't know any," Grandma said. "Don't be so restless, my lad, and listen to my tale."

It was close upon eleven o'clock at night when the performance began. The sovereign and his wives reclined at ease against their silk cushions on the divans. The maharaja sat at the center, with the queens to his right; the maharani, the highest-ranking woman, occupied a seat next to her consort. The courtesans took their places on his left.

Talented young women enacted the story of Dhruva for almost two hours. Costume colors like uniforms, distinguished each troupe. The maharani's dancers shimmered in pale gold, the second queen's artistes glided in mauve, while the third rani's team pirouetted in eggshell blue, and finally, the fourth royal's group swayed in the hues of freshly-sprouted banana leaves. Their attire consisted of form-fitting blouses and ankle-length, flowing skirts gathered tightly at the waist. A long, filmy stretch of cloth draped their coiffed heads and bosoms.

The episodes in the play of Suruchi's jealous rage at her step-son Dhruva, the child's tears and search for solace from his mother, Suniti, and his eventual banishment into the forest; later, seeing the vision of Lord Narayana in the woods—all these scenes were part of the drama. Court musicians and singers accompanied the rendition.

The royal personages as well as the invitees gazed in rapt attention at the series of tableaux.

Around this time, food began arriving from the kitchens. Eunuchs and maids stepped forward with silver salvers filled with thirty to forty minuscule bowls or *katori*s containing many kinds of curried vegetables and placed them on low tables set before the sovereign and his wives. Pilaf and puffed fried breads lay on each platter as well. Puddings and sweets came in separate dishes. There were so many scrumptious things to eat, most beyond the wildest dreams of ordinary folk.

The king periodically nibbled at the savories, all the while observing the dancers and making an occasional remark to the maharani.

Crimson streaks rippled across the eastern sky. Nightingales, nestled inside golden cages, trilled, and cockatoos, tied by their feet to long silver chains, rustled their wings. Richly-plumed peacocks, roosting on the rooftop gardens, awoke to another day with their haunting cries. The oil lamps flickered and dimmed, and still the dancers danced.

In the flowerpots nearby, buds burst open in the cool morning air. Suddenly, the sun emerged from the rose-blushed clouds hanging thick over the hills.

Eyes heavy with sleep, the royals watched the finale, as one by one each danseuse approached their majesties, made their deep obeisances and, still facing them, walked backwards out of the courtyard.

The maharaja sat lost in thought. All of a sudden, he asked his queen, "Where did you get that singer?"

"Which one?"

"The one who played the part of Suniti?"

"My father bought her for me when she was a young girl, and has just begun learning some intricate steps."

"She is a pretty thing. And dances too?" The king paused for a moment. "What is her name?"

A frown creased his wife's brow. "Kesar."

The monarch, oblivious to his consort's displeasure, cleared his throat. "She sings beautifully. If you will lend her to me, she can give voice lessons to some of my courtesans."

The lady remained silent. Then she turned and faced him. "Why, your favorite, Sumeru, is most accomplished, she can teach your women just as well as Kesar can."

A thin film of perspiration appeared on the ruler's upper lip. "Well, I mean, um—but this girl has even better vocal chords."

His companion lowered her eyes and remained silent for a long moment. "No, you may not have her."

Her husband refrained from further comment. The maharani was a king's daughter, and by both birth and breeding, no less his equal.

The festivities came to a close. The principal consort took her customary leave of the sovereign and his retinue and retired to her chambers.

"Then what happened?" the children proclaimed. Some among them asked, "Why didn't she give him the girl?"

The storyteller smiled and shrugged. "Who knows why?"

Weeks went by, until one day the maharani came down with a high fever. Illness was a frequent visitor to the harem, as the queens in particular, received little or no exercise. This time, however, the afflictions were indeed severe and the lady lay prostrate for over a month. Her co-wives visited on occasion, and she was always surrounded by solicitous ladies-in-waiting. The ruler, however, busy with his own pleasures and pursuits, did not once stop by; his courtesans beguiled him for hours.

Sumeru was the king's favorite and she, by clever manipulation, now reigned supreme over all his concubines.

There came a time when the maharaja tired of his paramour. Her songs no longer bewitched him. Openly critical, he sent for Kesar.

At that time, the young woman was massaging the maharani's feet. She loved the queen and had known no other life. Raised from childhood as a personal maid to her mistress when she was still a princess, Kesar had accompanied the new bride upon her marriage to the maharana. The aide had blossomed into womanhood in the palace, and the simple Vrindavani print cotton sari she wore could not conceal her stunning beauty. Nearly twenty-five, with a complexion that glowed like a *champa* flower in the light of dawn, and with clouds of dark hair, the damsel looked up as one of the eunuchs arrived with the summons.

The reclining woman glanced at the messenger. "Yes, please go on ahead. I will send her along shortly."

The sovereign's wife gazed at her masseuse. "Kesar?"

The attendant, troubled by the royal command, sat with eyes downcast.

"How about it?" the august lady asked.

The listener's head drooped. "Please keep me with you. I don't want to leave your service."

"I'm afraid that cannot be. This is the third time that His Majesty has requested your company. I dare not refuse any further, lest I enrage him."

Habitually obedient to regal requests, the helper gave a deep sigh, bowed and took leave.

Kesar moved into the king's harem the following afternoon. Over the next several days, she began schooling his ladies in the finer points of music. Within weeks it was rumored in the women's pavilion that the newcomer's voice and charm had so captivated the monarch that he had eyes only for her, and had lost interest in even his closest concubines. Their dance and song had long since palled; the coy gestures had ceased to beguile him. Word further spread that the favorites, Sumeru, Kumeru, Sundar and Lakshmi, were furious.

One evening, as dusk was falling, a paler and thinner Kesar arrived at the maharani's abode. All the ladies-in-waiting gazed at her with curiosity; she had metamorphosed from mere maid to courtesan. Attired in silk and brocade, flashing jewelry from head to toe, she had returned to the place of her childhood. With one sweeping gesture, she discarded her jewels, wrapped a faded Vrindavani sari around herself and, head bowed, she slowly entered the room.

A faint smile creased the royal consort's face. "What has happened? You are so thin! How were you able to get leave to visit me?"

"The maharaja has gone hunting today, so I slipped away."

"With consent, I hope?"

"Whose permission? The king will be at his shikar lodge for several days."

The young woman's former employer thought for a moment. "Why didn't you ask the beloved Sumeru?"

The visitor gave a toss of her head. "I do not take orders from fellow concubines. The only commands I follow are those of Your Majesty or His Majesty."

Kesar's family, though poor, had been of proud heritage and had given her as a mere child to the palace. Descended from the warrior clan, raised among princesses, she was not one to readily humble herself except before royalty.

The maharani sat up. "Oh please, stop. Return immediately, and don't come back. It can be dangerous for you."

Kesar's eyes swam. "Do not send me back, I want to stay here and serve you. Please grant me refuge."

Eyes glistening, the queen, although saddened by her helper's obvious distress, held firm. She knew only too well the seriousness of the girl's offense. No female had the right to move freely within the premises.

Darkness descended and stars twinkled in the indigo sky. Like a grey ghost, the reluctant courtesan silently stole away through the dimly lit corridors to the apartments which she shared with the king's concubines.

The women residing in the cloistered precincts glanced at each other in surprise. Some among them gave each other surreptitious nudges, and others winked.

The maharani was fast asleep in her marble villa. Around three o'clock in the morning, she awoke in a cold sweat and screamed. "Saraswati?"

A maid who had fallen into a doze while massaging the queen's nether limbs, awoke with a start. Other ladies of the bedchamber slumbered in adjoining suites.

All the women crowded into the boudoir. "Is anything the matter, Your Majesty?" "Is Your Majesty not feeling well?"

The alarmed woman rubbed her eyes. "Did Kesar come to visit us just now?"

The aides exchanged puzzled looks.

The queen frowned and half rose. "Ask Lakshmi and Gauri to come here."

The two senior-most ladies-in-waiting arrived and stood in respectful concern by the agitated lady.

The maharani, her bosom heaving, pointed toward the rooftop garden. "Take a look and see if she is there."

By this time, nearly all the attendants had risen, and they crowded onto the terrace which lay ethereal in the moonlight. Citrus trees and flowering shrubs in enormous planters stood at intervals, where by day tame peacocks wandered in a flash of indigo and turquoise. The many-hued, long-tailed birds slept among the bushes and no sound emerged from the still bowers save the gentle splash of the water fountain. A bathhouse, concealed by masses of plants, stood behind the ornamental structure.

The monarch's wife clutched at her heart. "I saw Kesar standing behind the orange bush near the bathing room. She raised her arms, pressed her palms together and greeted me with a 'namaste'. She even seemed to say something, though I couldn't quite follow what was said. Surely, she cannot have left so soon?"

Moved by the queen's obvious distress, all the aides, lanterns in hand, searched among the profusion of foliage. Their endeavors proved fruitless. Nobody was near the cascading waters or anywhere in the vicinity.

"We found no one there. Ma'am may have imagined it," they said.

The unnerved lady sank back against her pillows and thought for a moment. "Perhaps it was a dream."

Saraswati nodded. "Yes, it must have been." She came forward and laid a hand on the regal feet. "Your Majesty will feel much better if I give you a foot rub. It is very cold tonight."

Morning arrived; the royal awoke from an uneven sleep. Workers had been up at dawn, sweeping and mopping the floors and preparing for another day. The queen glanced out of the latticed window overlooking the courtyard and saw clusters of women strangely subdued.

Lakshmi and Gauri, both ashen-faced, came forward and broke the news gently to their mistress. There had been a terrible accident the previous night. The oil lamps in Kesar's suite had overturned, and the girl and her roommates had burned to death.

The maharani sat immobile on her fine-spun sheets. She uttered no sound. Slowly, she turned her face away. A single thought stabbed through her brain—which nameless, faceless emissary had crept into that room in the dead of night and torched their silk-beribboned braids?

Tears coursed down her cheeks as she lay swathed in her silks and enmeshed in her glittering powerlessness.

Grandma ended the story.

Nalini's eyes widened. She drew in a sharp breath and wound a long pigtail around her right hand. Her voice trembled a little. "Tell us more. Wh-what actually happened?"

A young granddaughter looked up. "Did the rani really see Kesar's ghost that night?"

"Who knows? Now run along, I need my rest."

The Taint
Lalji Saheb

The young boy had been the king's son but not a prince; his mother, Surupa Rai, was the bewitching courtesan who had sung and danced her way to the maharaja's heart. She had been given the coveted title, *pashowanji,* and the lavishness of her apartments rivaled that of the maharani's. Although her rank in the nuanced palace hierarchy was below that of the principal consort, it was almost on par with that of the three wedded queens. She was indeed a star in the harem firmament and her looks, talent and grace outshone all other women.

Today was the child's funeral. At his sudden death, the anguished father ordered obsequies fit for a prince. It was not the custom to grieve thus for a concubine's offspring, but Sujan Singh, like his beautiful mama, had been a particular favorite of the king.

A special durbar was held to mourn his passing. Men from the nobility and aristocracy and all ranking courtiers arrived to pay their respects. Wearing white tunics, trousers and turbans, their heads bowed, they sat in silence in the hall decorated with tubs of pale blossoms. The wives of the noblemen and prosperous businessmen came in shrouded carriages, stepped out heavily veiled and were guided into the harem by the eunuchs. This section of the palace by contrast, was not soundless. Groups of women had been hired for a continuous display of sorrow, with repeated beating of the breast and high-pitched wailings. The maids and ladies-in-waiting were in tears, as the youngster had been a loveable child. By both tradition and custom, the mother remained in seclusion.

News of the untimely demise came to the ears of the British Resident in the kingdom. As the chargé d'affaires of Her Majesty, Queen Victoria, he was thrown into a quandary. According to English custom, one did not mourn the passing of a royal bastard at a state funeral. The maharaja's sorrow was real no doubt, but as representative of the Hanoverian ruler, overlord to the Rajputs, he pondered on the correct course of action. Nevertheless, he ordered his horse-drawn carriage and made his way to the palace. He entered the hall that was shrouded in pearl-white silk and approached the sovereign who sat at the far end, clasping his surviving son, Samar Singh, by the same courtesan. The dewan, or prime minister, stood beside them.

The envoy duly bowed before the king, then reached out and shook his hand. He sat on the chair pulled out for him by an aide and stared straight ahead. Discomfited by the display of grief but outwardly unperturbed, he fixed his eyes on the middle distance and talked of the weather, news from Whitehall and sundry affairs of state, but not once did he commiserate with his host on his recent loss.

The king drew the ten-year-old closer to him. "This is my son, Samar, and it was his younger brother who died a few days ago."

The stripling, his dark eyes bright with curiosity, gazed at the diplomat who had hair the color of freshly-harvested sheaves of wheat and eyes as transparent as marbles. At an imperceptible signal from the premier, the boy stepped forward and bowed.

The British Resident sat in silence: he did not acknowledge the presence of the child with even a word or gesture.

Samar had been taught that European greetings differed from those of Rajputs, and that if an Englishman extended his hand, he too, must extend his own. Eager to display his new-found knowledge, he shyly proffered his right arm to the guest, who sat immobile. Only after a vigorous shaking of the *dewan*'s head did the boy realize his folly, and stumbled back and stood between his all-powerful father and the learned prime minister, puzzled that, although adored by all in the palace, he did not even merit a glance from this foreign visitor.

The years slid by. The old king passed away; among his offspring there were many still living, while others had been felled by disease. The crown prince ascended the throne, and the children the maharaja had fathered with his courtesans had been apportioned property and gifts and their marriages arranged with sons and daughters of concubines from neighboring kingdoms. A huge, spreading family tree ran almost on parallel tracks as the direct royal lineages, the branches and tendrils well-interlaced, but all claiming descent from a paternal regal ancestor. Petty rivalries, jealousies and intrigues were rife among them and childlessness was resolved by either second or third marriages, or by adoption. Property could pass only through the male heir, so families with all daughters frenziedly sought baby boys of similar background to adopt. The first-born son inherited all the assets, while the younger brothers remained, to a greater or less extent, dependent on their eldest's largesse. Their lives mirrored that of the maharajas and they too were inculcated in the manly virtues and were schooled in the traditional pursuits of riding, hunting and siring heirs in their harems.

Upon the death of the old king, young Samar Singh, titled Lalji Saheb, received his share of land, and as the son of the favorite courtesan, his acreage was somewhat more than that of his half-brothers. His marriage had been arranged with a concubine's daughter from a nearby kingdom, and in his mansion and grounds there was room not only for his extended family and servants, but also for his mistresses—skilled dancers from the village who were housed in a separate area.

He led the leisured life of a man of property and over the course of years, his wife bore him four sons and two daughters. He named his male offspring after the sun, moon, stars and ocean: Surya Singh, Chandra Singh, Tara Singh and Samudra Singh. A doting father, he saw his girls twice a day, as they would greet him and run back to their nannies in the women's quarters. His boys he saw rather more, as he liked to gather them around him at mealtimes and they all ate in convivial silence broken by an occasional remark while the servants ladled out pilaf and piquant curries onto a myriad silver bowls on their large brass platters. From time to time guests would be invited to lavish dinners as the dancers performed their intricate routines to entertain them.

One evening as dinner came to a close Lalji Saheb, his face careworn, drew his oldest son aside. "How is the baby?"

Surya, married to a daughter of a royal concubine, had recently become a father. His eyes widened. He had observed of late that at times heavy frowns creased his father's brow but if anyone approached, the lines would vanish. The debonair dad he had known as a child, who could shoot deer with ease, was now a man well past his prime given to absent-minded stares and ponderous ruminations.

The servants came in to clear up and, stacking the plates and dishes on a tray, departed in a clatter.

Lalji Saheb turned to his younger sons and then faced Surya again. "I am getting on in years. My days are coming to a close. I am concerned about the future of your brothers. Your two sisters I was able to marry off well, the dowries paid were generous."

All the boys looked at their father, their faces alert. The eldest, an astute young man, sat with his head bent and glanced at his parent through half-closed eyes.

"How about if I carve out some acreage from our large holdings for your brothers? Perhaps I can build a small dwelling for each of them?"

"Please feel free to do as you wish," Surya said.

The old man sank back on his seat relieved. "I will make the necessary arrangements tomorrow."

At daybreak, Lalji Saheb thought otherwise. How could he, a mere mortal, even contemplate changing the laws of inheritance that had remained intact for centuries, when the kings themselves who claimed descent from the heavens honored the same rules? Cocooned in wealth, cloistered in his walled gardens, surrounded by servants and sycophants, he knew little of the workaday world, but concern for his sons' well-being gnawed at his heart.

The following week he called out to his boys to join him in the jasmine-scented garden to discuss an equitable distribution of assets, his eyes resting on each of them in turn. Although he loved them all, he was fondest of his youngest, Samudra. The eldest among them, heir to all property, cleverly remained silent during the conversation. The patriarch's voice tailed off after a while. He sighed in despair, lapsed into gloom and the discussion ended.

One summer evening, an elated Samudra returned from school and informed his father that he had not only passed his matriculation examination, he had done rather well. Lalji Saheb rose and embraced him. In their entire clan no one had yet passed the test, let alone excel. All the boys in their extended family were schooled in the proper pursuits befitting young gentlemen of leisure: riding, hunting, shooting and, at a later age, of hosting extravagant parties where food was ample, drink flowed freely and talented dancers charmed the guests. They learned their mother tongue, Hindi, and a smattering of Urdu, but no serious effort was expected of them as their secretaries were there to do all the work necessary to manage their estates.

"I want to throw a grand feast to celebrate the good news, but times are a little hard now. There has been some shortfall in crops this year and the taxes have risen as the English have levied additional fees on our kingdom," the father said.

"It does not matter," Samudra said.

His brothers and cousins streamed into the courtyard from their rooms and offered their congratulations tinged with envy.

"You are the youngest, yet you are the first in our family to pass," said one.

"Only the Thakur Saheb's sons go in for higher education. Some of them even learn English," remarked another.

Conversation continued until the stars appeared in the evening sky and the aroma of dinner in the final stages of preparation wafted into the courtyard. The relatives left and father and son were alone once again.

"Have you given your mother the good news?" asked Lalji Saheb.

"No, not yet. The Thakur Saheb of Shivgarh's third son, the Thakur Saheb of Amarpur's nephew, the grandsons of Tejgarh's Rao Saheb have all passed the matriculation exam, and are planning on attending Mayo College in Ajmer. Please, father, let me go there."

"You want more education? Of what use will it be to you?"

His son sat with head bowed, his chin in his palm. "None of us is a first-born, we are all younger siblings, and we have to fend for ourselves. If we do not get an education, we will never be able to obtain a well-paying position. With training we might be able to get a job, if not in our kingdom, then certainly elsewhere."

The old man was astonished. Samudra had always been an introspective child, but he had on his own been exploring various future options. Unfamiliar with the world of academia he asked, "What exactly is it that you wish to study at Ajmer?"

"I want to go there for the Intermediate Arts program, and if I pass, then onto a bachelor's degree."

"Hmm. Your friends from Tejgarh, Shivgarh and Amarpur are all going there? Well, let me make inquiries."

July was soon upon them. The torrential monsoons bathed the parched fields and transformed them into sheets of green and term was due to begin. In haste, Lalji Saheb sent his secretary to the local college for the requisite papers.

One morning when Samudra approached his father he learned that he had been admitted to the institution in their own town after all.

"Let us see how you fare over here, we can discuss where you will pursue your bachelor's degree later."

In the courtyard, the brothers, cousins and uncles conversed among themselves, weighing the relative merits of various programs. The student walked past them, quickly turning his head away to hide tears of anger and disappointment.

Samudra passed all the qualifying tests to the bemused wonder and delight of his father who obtained application forms from the local college once again. When the paperwork arrived, Lalji Saheb presented them to his son with some diffidence, fearing an outright refusal, for was it not the youth's ardent wish to attend the institution in Ajmer? To his surprise, the teenager acquiesced and duly filled out the required documents. Perhaps the boy has forgotten all about Mayo, thought the elder man with relief.

The young man began his educational pursuits. A quiet reflective boy, he excelled in his work, but almost overnight all his childhood friends had vanished, some to Ajmer and others to colleges elsewhere. He was left with classmates but no friends.

A spectacular celebration at Lalji Saheb's mansion marked the day the youth received his bachelor's degree. A feast was held to which virtually all the townsfolk were invited. Troupes of dancers and their accompanying musicians were hired for day-long performances. The large kitchen was abustle with frenetic activity from dawn to well past midnight, the cooks preparing mounds of fragrant pilaf, curries and rose-scented rice puddings. Huge earthenware vessels brimming with gulab-jamuns, jalebis and other delectable sweetmeats arrived from the confectioners in town. The entire house resounded to the laughter of the assembled guests. The ladies, dressed in crimson, blue and yellow silks which shimmered as they moved, thronged to the secluded inner courtyard, whilst the men congregated and conversed in the outer. *Purdah* was maintained in Lalji Saheb's house, the food being served to women and children in an enclosure separate and distinct from where the men enjoyed their meal. A special ceremony was also held and propitious offerings were made at the temple.

Word spread to the neighboring kingdoms about the scholar's laurels. Marriage proposals poured in on behalf of daughters of kings and their concubines. To the joy of Lalji Saheb, these teenaged girls were not mere descendants of long-dead rulers, but children of royal blood. The old man breathed a sigh of relief; his son would be freed from the dependent status assigned to younger sons, and his dowry would go a long way to keep him from want.

Bursting with pride, the father began marriage negotiations in earnest. Weddings and funerals were the stuff of life, and he was duty-bound to see that his children's futures were assured. The question of consulting his son about the impending nuptials did not arise. He had heard that in some distant parts, young people had some say in choosing their lifelong companions, but that custom was not prevalent in his town, and besides, he as a parent with the wisdom of years, knew what was best.

One winter night, Samudra came to his father's room. It was late and all the servants had gone to bed. Lalji Saheb, reclined on his bed and wrapped in a silk quilt, was reading aloud to himself from the Hindi version of the *Bhagavad Gita*. His children, the domestic help and other members of his large household often gathered around him, sitting on woven mats to hear words of wisdom from the *Gita*. At this late hour he was alone. Seeing his son at the doorway, he closed his book and motioned the boy to come inside, away from the icy chill.

Samudra, with a golden complexion and curling hair, resembled his grandmother the most. The courtesan, a woman of stunning beauty, a dancer of rare talent and the maharaja's darling, had bequeathed her looks to her youngest grandchild. The old man glanced at the visitor in mild surprise as it was rather late, even for members of their extended family. The boy had his grandma's smile, but it was his dark, expressive eyes that reminded Lalji Saheb of his own mother.

The youth came in and sat at his father's bedside, asked after his health and made a few desultory remarks. "I have found a job," he said at last. "I was not able to seek your permission earlier since you had been unwell. Indeed, I had thought that I might not be able to accept the job after all."

His father, recumbent on his divan, sat up. "You have found work? Where? In this town I hope. Who gave it to you?"

The Second World War had entered its second year.

"No, not here, I have found a position in the military. I sent in my application some time ago."

The old man, his face grey and lined, stared at his son. "What's that? A job, fighting? What kind of work? Is it transportation or the mess? Or, are you a captain? Those are all very good commissions, but you can get them here in our own city, why not try our maharaja's forces?"

"No, those kinds of prestigious positions are not given to us. Only the Rajput chieftains and their sons are entitled to them," his son said. "You know that too, father." He paused for a moment. "I am getting a job in the army in British India. They are actively enlisting. A number of young men from our kingdom have already left." He looked away and stared at the floor.

His father gazed at his son's averted face, wondering whether to be pleased or fearful. What exactly did fighting entail nowadays? Would his offspring be able to shoulder his responsibilities? Where would he be sent? These thoughts raced through his brain.

"Is it a job like Comedanjee's?" he asked. He had known a warrior who had cut an impressive figure astride his horse, sporting his magnificent spear and later a rifle, and had seen service not only in the kingdom, but also had fought in the Boer Wars. As a boy, Lalji Saheb had listened wide-eyed to the vivid tales of Africa, till the acrid smell of gun smoke, the roars of lions in the veldt and the whinnying shrieks of chargers locked in mortal combat seemed more real to him than the rolling hills of Rajputana.

His son laughed. "No, commander-in-chief is a very high position. Nowadays, people don't fight with swords, spears or *trishuls*. Upon old Comedanjee's retirement, there were many changes in the army. My position is very modest, I have joined the infantry."

"Which country will you be fighting in, then?"

"At first they are sending us to a training camp in Mhow. After that, they could send us anywhere, Assam, Burma, or somewhere else."

A man of moderate learning but of immense wealth, Lalji Saheb sat upright on his divan and stared at his son. His knowledge of geography was akin to that of the royal concubines, so minuscule was his information about the world outside.

"When will you return?" he said.

"Whenever I manage to get leave."

The father frowned. "I will make every effort to find you something locally. Please don't make any hasty decisions."

Samudra glanced at the far wall. A fresco of vines and flowers met his gaze where birds of brilliant plumage nested in the verdant foliage. His eyes slid to the painted surface of a low table where kings and princes perched on elephants' brocaded backs sallied forth on an eternal royal hunt, the striped, tawny beasts fleeing ahead. On one wall hung a portrait of his august grandfather in ceremonial robes, 'and adjacent was a picture of the present ruler,' his father's half-brother. A photograph of King George V and Queen Mary posing with their brood, and a small framed picture of the current English emperor and his bride occupied a smaller, less prominent section of the wall. A few European landscapes were also scattered around the room.

He turned his head and saw his face in the gilt-edged mirror of beveled glass, and saw too, the reflection of a portrait of his father as a young man attired in riding clothes, a silver-handled whip in his hand as though venturing out on a hunt, his proud eyes flashing beneath a bejeweled turban. Two imported clocks chimed the hour.

Samudra turned around and faced his father. "No, not here."

"Why not? Let me try to get you a job, if not in this town, at least in our own country."

"You will not be able to get me anything decent here, and you know well enough why. It is for that reason alone I was not able to go to Mayo, and that is also why I will never be able to get a remunerative position here." The young man paced the room.

His father bowed his head and remained silent for a while. "How did you know? Did you ask someone?"

The youth stared once again at the far wall, recalling a long-ago conversation he had had with a friend.

"It will be wonderful when we all go to Ajmer, won't it?" young Samudra had said.

"You will never be able to attend the college there."

"Why not? I have done so well in my entrance exams, and my dad has promised to send me to Mayo."

His friend had given him a furtive glance, pursed his lips and had said no more.

He recounted this conversation to his father.

A deep flush rose from the back of Lalji Saheb's neck, mottled his cheeks and crept up to the temples. Tiny droplets appeared above his upper lip. The book slipped and lay half open on the bed. He grabbed one end of the coverlet in his fist and frowned. His voice had a metallic timbre. "Then what else did you learn?"

"When he returned from Ajmer during his holidays after his Intermediate Arts finals, and I too had passed the very same exam at our local college, I went to him to get information about entering Mayo for my bachelor's degree. He told me that I would never be able to gain admission there.

This time I pressed him for an answer. He was embarrassed at first and then he told me that Mayo College at Ajmer was for the children of kings and nobility, not for half-bloods like me. His grandfather, a prince at Tejgarh, had told him that the place was only for royalty and their rightful descendants and heirs. In fact, his own beloved concubine's sons, who were raised and educated in the same household and were my friend's playmates, were forever barred from that place. It is also an institution founded by the English in our kingdom, so even if Rajputs can be flexible, British custom prevails over there.

"My grandfather, your father, was a king, but I descend from his concubine, not his queen."

Lalji Saheb listened in silence, while a shard of memory splintered through his brain. A boy, enveloped in the fond embrace of his papa, approaching the British Resident Saheb; his hurt and bewilderment at being so utterly ignored, he who was adored by the king as well as the courtiers. Something else stirred in his mind too, a memory of a conversation with a friend who was the son of one of the many palace functionaries. When just out of their teens, his companion had told him that although an adored child of the king, he was not on par with the princes. It had come as a shock to him to learn that his mother, a dancer of renown who had stolen the maharaja's heart and ranked just below the queens, was nothing more than a mere concubine. According to Rajput custom they would be well-provided for, but the English were spreading their net far and wide over India, and they did not recognize royal courtesans. That alone had accounted for his reluctance in pursuing Mayo on his son's behalf as he had wished to spare him disappointment and heartache.

The night wore on, a thick mist pressed against the windowpanes, the minutes ticked by and the clocks struck the hour.

"I have arranged a most wonderful match for you. The bridal trousseau alone is worth a king's ransom, not to speak of the dowry. Cases of gold mohurs have been promised, you will never experience want. If you must go, why don't you get married and then leave?" Lalji Saheb said.

Custom decreed that the first-born male inherit all property, but he as a father could help assure his younger sons' futures by arranging advantageous marriages. Besides, he couldn't bear the thought of his children not being near him. The brothers and their families, though their fortunes dwindled, all remained to a greater or lesser extent dependent on their eldest male sibling as part of a vast extended family, performing familial roles and various duties.

The young man's eyes wandered around the room. He saw an indolent man but an affectionate father shrouded in a silk quilt sitting on his cushioned bed living a life of great ease on inherited wealth that he could not bequeath.

"Even if the dowry was worth countless rupees, my wife, though a king's daughter would still be the child of a concubine. Our children will be Darogas, not Rajputs, and will remain forever removed from any position of power, even if our oldest son manages to live in fair comfort from his inheritance," Samudra said.

He fixed his father with a look. "I think you know that too." He paused. "If I had not received an education, I probably would not feel it so keenly. But when I passed my Intermediate Arts exam with flying colors, and then was prevented from attending Mayo College, my only desire now is to achieve what I can."

"But the girl's dowry is worth a solid fortune. You can live in undreamed of luxury all your life. I have also heard that she is very beautiful, and a beguiling dancer, too. Why can't you just be happy about it? So what if you cannot get a challenging position in the royal army like a Rajput, you will still be amply provided for. This is the way it has always been, it is our tradition."

Scattered thoughts scurried around in the old man's brain. *If only I had not allowed him an education, he would have been content with his lot in life. The money alone would tempt any young man; what can he be thinking of? Having tasted from the tree of knowledge, the youth has developed an unseemly desire for forbidden fruit.* He dared not voice his feelings but sat still and searched his son's face.

"At this point in time, father, I cannot accept this girl's hand. With your permission, I plan on accepting a job in the army in British India."

Lalji Saheb jerked up his head. "What? But you cannot simply leave—I am arranging your marriage—her family—their wealth—" His eyes glistened. Then he dropped his head in his hands.

Outside, the fog eddied and swirled, shrouding the mansion in widow's white; indoors sat father and son in frozen silence, both blessed and tainted by their royal blood.

Samudra rose, bowed to his parent, took his leave and then vanished into the misty night.

Ungendered

Khushanjarji

The maharaja's birthday was fast approaching; preparations were afoot on a lavish scale in the royal harem. The queen mothers, all widows of the former sovereign, doted on the young ruler and each took pains to plan a grand feast for him. The maharani, his principal consort, with the help of her ladies-in-waiting, was absorbed in planning the many dances to be performed in her villa to honor and fete the king. The lesser queens, the ranis, were no less eager to please their husband and daily, their apartments reverberated to the beat of drums, clink of hand cymbals and the tinkle of ankle bells as their troupes of dancers practiced by the hour. The king's favorite concubines too, organized and planned to the minutest detail festivities to beguile and flatter their lover. Each queen and courtesan ordered a delectable dinner be prepared in the royal kitchens on the day of his visit; the birthday celebrations, according to custom, would continue for almost a week.

The responsibility for helping organize the many events fell on the shoulders of the chief eunuch. The lean grey-haired man, accompanied by his son, walked down the corridors of the harem and from each queen's abode emerged a long list of desired items to be delivered to her villa at an appointed day and time, no less. The royal ladies and all the maids addressed the eunuch as Khushanjarji, a title which had been conferred by the king, although his real name was Allabaksh. The title itself meant 'one who pleaseth' and, during the course of his life, he had indeed performed many duties, some pleasant and some undesirable, to please his master. The sole male permitted entry into the pavilion of women, he alone knew of its innermost secrets.

He sped from villa to apartment and mused on the fate of a handful of women. There were indeed some whose charms had captivated the king and whom by royal command he had escorted to his chambers, but there were others yet, who had fallen afoul of either the king or his mistress of the moment; they had been incarcerated in the nether regions of the palace, with their days numbered. Over the years, he had won the trust and approval of the king and had been rewarded with titles, gifts and a *jaigir* of an annual sum of three thousand rupees. He mused that perhaps during the king's birthday celebrations, he might receive the coveted royal title, Tazimi Sirdar, the highest honor conferred to a commoner.

He left the maharani's villa, armed with a long list and entered the dowager queen's suite and took orders for flowers and traditional sweets for the ceremony, and made rapid mental calculations as to the number of vats of golden-brown gulab jamuns swimming in syrup that would be needed. He knocked on the doors of the next set of apartments occupied by the remaining queen mothers and once again received requests for fruits, flowers and confectionery. Moving at a brisk pace, he arrived at the residences of the ranis and their attendants and took their orders as well.

He ventured farther through the dimly lit corridors until he came to the doors of the king's favorite concubines. A handful of women, having attained the highest rank possible for mere commoners, enjoyed a lavish lifestyle within the confines of the harem. They had sung and danced their way to the maharaja's heart and had been granted the title Pashowan, while the lesser favorites but the king's darlings nonetheless, were titled Pardayet. They vied with each other for a second royal glance.

The eunuch paused and made a mental note of their varied requests. He was the first to learn which damsel among them was to be feted during the king's birthday celebrations and who would receive the desired Tazimi award and customary gold anklets; he was also the first to know or sense who would face an unhappy fate.

He navigated his way through the palace labyrinth and handed out the queens' invitations for the banquet to the many palace dwellers. His keen eyes saw curtains whisked aside, doors opening and closing farther down the hallway, a wisp of veil vanish around the corner and his ears caught the sound of subdued murmurs and sudden silences. A whiff of intrigue, a scent of scandal and Khushanjarji found himself drawn into the machinations of the women. They pleaded with him for news of certain concubines, trying to pry information using all their feminine wiles, but as guardian of the harem, he saw all, heard all, but remained tight-lipped.

Wherever he went, groups of girls clad in simple tunics and pantaloons gathered around him, gazing up at him with large kohl-rimmed eyes; raised in the palace from childhood to wait on the queens, they surrounded the eunuch. Some stroked his tunic, others reached up to hold his hand, while a handful gazed in wonder at his embroidered *nagra* shoes.

"What kind of food will be there at the feast?" they asked.

The nourishment served them he knew was ample, but plain. Any pageantry provided them a refreshing departure from their daily fare, so he embellished his description of the pilafs, vegetables in piquant sauces, milk puddings and golden orbs of gulab jamuns until he felt his own mouth water.

In a world where men were barred, the eunuch was a visitor from distant parts who brought news however insignificant, from the great outdoors. Life continued in a circadian rhythm save the occasional birth or death of a concubine's child, so any revelry was a source of merriment, intense curiosity and speculation.

The eunuch's son, a youthful stalwart, following his father some distance behind, was also mobbed by a clutch of chattering children. Teenagers dressed in swirling skirts, *choli* blouses and long scarves peeped out as the harem guardian walked past, but when they saw the approaching young man they threw their filmy scarves over their heads and hid behind the curtains. The elderly eunuch smiled at the quivering draperies. Doe-eyed young saplings they were, with lacy patterns of *mehndi* on their palms and feet, he knew that they were all virgins and that their sole function was to perform in tableaus for the queens—until they caught the maharaja's eye.

He rounded a corner and knocked on the door to the suite of one of the king's beloveds, and upon being bidden entry, he removed his shoes. Having handed the maharani's invitations, he returned to the entrance and stared at the floor, his mouth hanging open. His footwear had vanished. In its place was a pair of tiny red slippers. At the sound of suppressed laughter, he turned his head and saw the mischievous eyes of a girl, and in mock sternness he admonished her. She defied him with an airy insouciance and then flung the shoes at his feet and disappeared down the corridor in a squeal of giggles.

He gave an indulgent smile and continued on his way, but his progress was slow. Feminine voices echoed in the hallways.

"Khushanjarji, can you please get me some kohl for the eyes?" "I need more material to make a blouse." "Can I have more hair ribbons please, mine are old and frayed."

Some of the young women shied away from him like startled gazelles, fearful that they had overstepped the bounds of propriety, but he smiled upon them with utmost affection, answering all their questions and, whenever possible, acquiescing to their myriad demands.

Khushanjarji completed issuing all the invitations and as the day drew to a close, he and his son, Khudabaksh, walked along the dark alleyways that encircled the women's quarters. At intervals, huge lamps stood on top of the walls, the flames shedding a faint light on the path below, and high up were tiny grilles built into the walls. Circumambulating the harem, the eunuch came to a small verandah where he prostrated himself and said his prayers. His day was not yet done. He still had to visit the courtesan Prem Rai and take her orders.

Dusk was deepening and the eunuch walked in a measured tread along the walled passageway. Far ahead in the gathering gloom, he saw the flames from the lamps give a violent quiver; puzzled, he stood in the calm of the evening and caught a fleeting glimpse of a pink veil, large eyes and a laughing mouth. The vision vanished as quickly as it had come. He smiled a little, no doubt it was a young dancer from the courtesan's rooms, snatching a quick look or more likely, had some request for his ears alone.

He strode to the end of the corridor and to his surprise saw no one. He turned the corner and only bare walls and a deserted alley met his gaze. An oil lamp stood on top of the wall above his head and in the dim light, he turned towards his son. "Did you see anyone?"

"No, I did not," the young man said.

Khushanjarji paused. "Let's see if we can find the girl. Perhaps she is hiding somewhere. I thought I saw someone flitting away in the dark. Could it be Kaveri Bai? No, that cannot be."

His son looked around with energy and peered into the cracks on the walls. "No, nobody is here. In any case, the gate to the villa is still shut. No one will dare leave things unlocked without your permission."

An absent frown furrowed the old man's brow. "Yes, of course."

The door opened and Prem Rai's maid ushered in the two men.

A group of girls and women crowded around them, and murmured greetings. Khushanjarji responded with warmth while his eyes swept over them searching for a face, but try as he might, he still could not find the teenager with the pink veil.

The king's birthday arrived and was celebrated with due pomp and circumstance. Feasting continued well into the early hours of the morning while a steady stream of dancers pirouetted before the maharaja and his queens. A handful of beautiful young concubines, skilled in the arts, received royal honors and were promoted to the Pardayet status, while a cluster of girls entered *sakhidom*. Khushanjarji received the sought-after Tazimi award, wincing a little when the solid gold anklets were fastened on him; his son Khudabaksh was awarded a prize too, that of a gold brocade turban. The entire palace was engulfed in festivities from the apartments of the maharani to those of the concubines.

A few months went by and life in the palace went back to its time-honored routines.

A servant came and stood outside Khudabaksh's room. "Khushanjarji sends you his greetings and asks to see you."

Khudabaksh rose and went to his father's apartment. The weather was unseasonably warm; the *khus khus* screens had been spattered with water, and in the darkened bedroom, the old man lay on a raised bedstead of white marble. His hookah was placed to one side, and his turban rested on the edge of his bed. A servant stood behind, cooling him with a fan.

The young man bowed before his father. "*Abbajan,* are you not well?"

The eunuch gestured toward a chair. "I'm fine, my son."

Khushanjarji gazed in an unseeing manner at the visitor, a faint frown on his brow. His brocade slippers lay on the floor and could easily be mistaken for those of a girl's. Of slight build with a copper-colored face, there was little resemblance between him and his tall, well-built son. On the bed an open letter lay fluttering in the gentle breeze administered by the toiling servant as he wielded the fan with vigor.

"Do you remember your mother at all?" the father said.

"Yes, I do."

"You don't really know much about your mother. How she came to stay with me..." Khushanjarji's voice trailed off as he looked into his son's face.

The young man crinkled his forehead. "No, I suppose I don't."

"I first met your mother in Delhi. That was fifty years ago. His Majesty wanted to visit that city after his pilgrimage to Haridwar and Vrindavan. I had to go on ahead and make all the arrangements. The maharani was going too, and a handful of her ladies-in-waiting as well; so the responsibility for the entire trip, naturally, fell on my shoulders. You can imagine what a to-do that was. Strict *purdah* had to be maintained, so all the carriages had to be shrouded with curtains. I was quite young then, not much older than you." A smile lingered on the eunuch's lips.

"While making the preparations for the pilgrimage and tour, I ran into an old friend of mine near Delhi. He told me of your mother. She had been the wife of a distant cousin of theirs, but was recently widowed. She had a very young child with her, and was in dire straits." He paused and looked hard at Khudabaksh.

"You were that toddler. Your mother was young and attractive, but had no interest in marrying again. She had nowhere to stay and no one really wished to extend her anything more than temporary shelter. Other than owning a few pieces of jewelry, she was destitute. Your father had a store selling glassware, but upon his death that closed.

"Meanwhile, for a long time I had felt that my house needed a woman's touch. But what could I offer a lady, and what would her relationship be with me?" Khushanjarji stopped and almost choked on his words. He glanced at his son who sat before him with his head bent, listening in rapt attention, hands clasped over his knees.

"I have never told you how I came to be here. My family was very poor, and when I was but a mere child, a relative of ours saved the life of the then chief eunuch at this palace. Perhaps my uncle saved him from being attacked by a tiger at a royal shoot, I really don't know." The old man took a deep breath and fidgeted with a button on his tunic.

"I have very little memory of what followed. All I know is that out of gratitude, the eunuch offered to take one of us children to alleviate my family's distress. I cannot recall my mother's face or that of my father's. The only parent I have really known is the man who adopted me, the previous chief eunuch. He raised me in his house on the palace grounds, this very bungalow that you and I now live in. I was so very young then, that I cannot even recall at what point I was initiated into eunuchhood."

The heat in the room was stifling. An immobile Khudabaksh continued staring at the floor. The water carrier, or *bhisti,* came by and sprayed the green *khus khus* screens from his goatskin bag and a sudden, fresh breeze enveloped the two men in the room.

Khushanjarji stared at the far wall, lost in reverie. When he spoke again, the timbre of his voice had changed, it sounded thin and tired. "Well, that's past history. Now let me tell you about your mother. In our kind of household, it makes no sense to have a woman around. Who ever heard of a married eunuch? So I sent word through my friend explaining the whole situation, saying that I would offer her shelter, but could not provide marital bliss. I knew that she was destitute, and wished to help out an old friend by providing his extended family support. If she chose to live with me and manage my household, I would claim her as a distant relative and she would live with me as an equal, not a maid.

"I must confess my motives were not entirely altruistic. I had seen you with your mother once and wanted you. Why? Kings, princes, nobility, can bequeath their wealth to their sons and heirs, even the lowly peasant leaves his ploughs and plot for his progeny, but I, who have won the supreme trust of the king and am a person of wealth, can have no descendants—ever." The man's face flushed beneath his rich mahogany skin and he tugged at the buttons on his shirt till they ripped out, and clenched his left fist. "By the customs of the kingdom, however, even if I cannot have a son I can still have an heir. You were a fine-looking boy and would be an asset to any palace. Your mother was very poor, I knew, and believed that in time she would agree to my adopting you and have you follow in my footsteps.

"She could live in comfort all her life, since you would inherit my property and sizeable hoard of gold coins and continue to amass wealth of your own as a chief eunuch. Who can say no if flashing gems are dangled before their eyes?"

Khushanjarji paused and pulled at his hookah. The fire had gone out and he tried to smoke his pipe in vain. His son called out to the servant for more tobacco and with a touch of impatience told him to light it.

The afternoon drew to a close. The wind rose in the valley; the servant raised the *khus khus* screens to let in the southern breezes. Light flooded the room and the sun dipped behind the Aravalli hills. A rush of air swept over the moat around the castle and the atmosphere inside the room turned balmy.

The old man's voice dropped. "Your mother agreed to live with me as a make-believe relative and to my joy, I had the two of you. She was young, only twenty-two or three, and you were a toddler. Her name was Noor Nihar. She died rather unexpectedly, three years later from a brief illness. I had meant to ask her permission to adopt you, but had not the courage. What if she objected? So, I kept delaying matters and was indeed saddened by her death, but to my delight, found myself your sole guardian. At last you were mine."

The elderly eunuch avoided his listener's gaze; he had inflicted a grievous injury on his adopted son. His own desire for an heir had deprived the handsome youth of his manhood. In the stillness of the room, the only sound was that of the water trickling down the bamboo screens as the *bhisti* continued spraying from his goatskin bag.

Khudabaksh stared at the floor. He heard a crackle of paper in the faint breeze that had crept into the room and only then did he raise his head.

"Here is a letter from Gulsurat, one of your mother's distant relatives," Khushanjarji said. "She has two sons and has been recently widowed. They would like to come and stay with us. She arrives at the city tonight with her children, so please go meet the family and bring them here."

Khushanjarji's house resounded to the echoes of childish laughter. The staid environment of the eunuch's household was thrown in disarray. The home appeared enormous to the two boys fresh from their derelict rooms in Delhi and they scampered up and down the stairs, raced around playing hide-and-seek until they were called to order by their mother who was overwhelmed by her plush surroundings and the exuberance of her sons. Toys lay scattered, the children chattered non-stop, calling out "Grandpa" as the eunuch returned at day's end and swinging on his arm. In the old man's eyes, a sparkle appeared and he stooped less. His adoptee, Khudabaksh, whom Gulsurat respectfully addressed as Bhai Saheb, fell into the new routine and, in his spare time, ran around the garden, playing assorted games with the children.

Months went by and with each passing day, the harem guardian appeared increasingly feeble and began delegating most of his duties to his heir. Gulsurat, meanwhile, added a unique feminine touch to the home, evident in the daintiness of the floral arrangements and the array of delicacies for their meals. This was the first time in their young lives that her sons were able to eat wholesome food and she took great pride in preparing nourishing viands in her kitchen using only tender cuts of lamb, and the freshest vegetables and choicest grains.

One afternoon, Khushanjarji awoke from his nap and called out to his son. Khudabaksh was in the garden, enjoying the spring sunshine which was as yet still mellow, a prelude to the scorching haze of the summers. A light breeze rustled through the trees and the air was heavy with the fragrance of jasmine and roses. Scarlet hibiscus burst forth, flaring petals and long stamens from the profusion of bushes at the edge of the garden. The wind rippled through the boughs overhead, sending the sun-dappled leaves into an ecstasy; the young man strolling below breathed in the aroma of the flowers and felt his blood quicken as the warm air caressed his skin. Upon hearing his name, he was instantly at his father's bedside.

"Please sit down," Khushanjarji said. "Do you remember the maharaja's birthday? You and I went and handed out invitations. Do you recall the moment we came near Prem Rai's villa?"

"Yes, of course I do."

"Remember that pretty girl we saw slipping away? We both looked, but could not find her? Well, I saw her last night and not only that, I also recognized her."

Khudabaksh gaped at his father. Nobody from the harem had ever visited their house—so closely guarded were the women that every movement of theirs was monitored.

The elderly eunuch sat upright. "Her name is Godaveri Bai. I saw her in my dream last night, the pink wisp of veil, her pretty face, she was walking ahead of me. Suddenly, she veered to the left and disappeared down a flight of stairs and as she turned, I saw her face. All this time, I have often wondered who this girl was and why we could not trace her. Where had she hidden? Last night I realized that she did not hide herself. Yes, she was Godaveri Bai."

The son looked at his father with rising concern. The man was old and feeble, but was he also losing his grip on reality?

Khushanjarji paused and stared at the wall through rheumy eyes. "I had thought that I would be able to save her, but I could not."

He turned his head and gazed out of the window, his thoughts flying back over decades; a beautiful girl, part of Prem Rai's entourage, dancing during one of the palace revelries. The maharaja, glancing in her direction, had remarked on her exquisite grace. The following day the girl had been taken ill. She had been sequestered by maids and placed in seclusion in a ground floor room of the courtesan's villa. The royal doctor had been summoned and potions prepared and fed daily to the girl, but to no avail. After a brief illness, she died.

The eunuch had suspected that the healing concoctions had been laced with something else by the concubine's maids and had tried to plead her case but had been summarily dismissed.

Khudabaksh gazed at his father with apprehension; the old man's mind must be wandering. He could not possibly have seen anyone that night. Why, both of them had scoured the alley that evening for that slip of a girl; no doubt it had been the shadow of a vine on the centuries-old castle walls. He recalled with a twinge of unease that the flames from the oil lamp had quivered in a strange fashion in that still air, as though a being invisible to any mortal had quickly passed by.

Gulsurat came indoors, leaving her sons playing outside.

The old man smiled at the woman. "I have been thinking for some time now, that my days are coming to a close. That is why it is so good to have you all here with me. You probably know that when a royal eunuch dies, all his wealth reverts to the Crown. It is fairly obvious, is it not? After all, we can have no descendants. That is the reason why I was adopted, and that is also why I raised young Khudabaksh, so that he could carry on in my footsteps and moreover, inherit my entire *jaigir,* or property. I have also spent many a sleepless night pondering as to who might come next and get the booty after my heir passes on."

He stopped and looked at Gulsurat. "It was about this time that your letter arrived. I realized then, that you provided me with an easy solution."

Voices could be heard outdoors, as Haqiqat and Habib argued sundry points of a game with the robustness of youth.

The palace functionary turned towards the window and remained lost in thought. "Yes, I have a great deal of wealth, who could I leave it to—has been my main concern until now." His voice trailed off, and once again he stared out into the garden, then swung round to face the mother. "My dear, I have sensed that you too hope that I take one of your sons as a future heir."

The young woman's voice was soft. "As you please, sir."

"What about you, Khudabaksh, do you want an heir?" Khushanjarji said.

The young man sensed that for some reason that he could not yet fathom, his father seemed perturbed. "Whatever you desire, I will follow your advice," he replied.

"Tell Habib and Haqiqat to come in here," the old man said.

Khudabaksh left the room and returned with two breathless boys who scampered up to their mother.

The eunuch's eyes grew large as he gazed at Gulsurat and her sons. Bright-eyed, mischievous, with tousled locks falling over their foreheads, the two youngsters stood before him. He reached out and ran his gnarled finger down Haqiqat's cheek and ruffled the dark curls of Habib and said, "Run along now, go outside and play."

They fled outdoors, eager to continue with their games.

Khushanjarji looked at his heir. "Do you know what I have been thinking about all these days ever since our guests came to live with us? It would have been so wonderful if she could have been your bride and those two charming boys, your sons."

Khudabaksh hung his head and stared at the floor. Gulsurat's face turned crimson.

"Don't feel embarrassed my son. The dishonor is mine," the foster father said. He paused for a long moment and tugged at his earlobes, then turned to face the woman. "My dear, I have decided that I will not take your children."

Gulsurat gasped and stared open-mouthed at her host. A windswept mirage of dingy, tenement dwellings in the back alleys of Delhi flashed before her eyes.

The young man jerked up his head and looked out at their manicured garden and avoided his father's gaze.

"My days are numbered. I had initially thought that I would go ahead with the adoption, but no, I cannot."

The mother's bosom heaved and teardrops trembled on her eyelashes. "Why are you so hesitant, sir? I have two kids after all. Why don't you take one of them at least?"

The old man smiled. "I know that you have two sons, but they each have only one life to live. You will not be able to give them another life. Those good-looking, active youngsters deserve a normal life full of everyday human hopes and longing. If I took one of your children, would not his life change forever? Have I been able to give my adoptee all the joys that a man can ask for? Let your sons attain manhood like other boys. If they remain poor, so be it—but at least they will be men. It was only my pride that demanded an heir."

Laughter could be heard outside. "Catch me if you can"—"No, you didn't"—"Yes I did," and amidst all that, loud chuckles, as the boys played their games in wild abandon.

The eunuch sat on his bed, eyes downcast, as waves of childish mirth wafted in through the window.

In a corner of the room, an ashen-faced Gulsurat stood in frozen silence.

The Courtesan's Tale
Sumeru Rai

Faint streaks of flame rippled across the pale sky. The young woman stepped onto the dew-laden grass and walked towards the cowshed; the door was ajar.

She paused and glanced at her widowed mother-in-law who sat on her reed mat on the front porch. "Did you forget to lock up last night?" Without waiting for a reply, she entered the building. "Who is that lying down over there?"

The matriarch frowned. "Why are you causing all this commotion so early in the morning? At first you said that I hadn't latched the door, but I distinctly recall that I had done so last night. Now you are saying that someone is hidden there. What's going on?"

Her sons, roused from their sleep, came outside. The young woman, upon seeing her husband with his younger brother, covered her head with her long scarf and glanced at her spouse. "Why don't you go and see who is inside?"

The two men, both annoyed and curious, entered the little barn followed by their wives.

The elder of the two women ventured into its dark recesses and peered into the gloom. "Oh, it is your sister, Umda Bai!"

To one side sat some cows and their wide-eyed calves, and at the farther end stood the large grinding stone. A teenager lay asleep near the wheat grinder; her blue veil had slipped from her head and spread out on the dusty floor while the red ribbon that had anchored her braids was untied. The sleeping woman wore a crimson blouse and a rather dirty yellow ankle-length skirt. A *hasuli* choker gleamed on her throat, a *tikli* sat askew on her hair and from her ears dangled gold earrings. Through the slats of the doorway, the sunbeams fell on her feet and the silver anklets dazzled in the light. Umda Bai stirred, sat up and gazed bleary-eyed at those assembled.

Tej Singh, the elder of the two men, strode inside the shed. "Where have you come from?"

"With whom did you arrive? And why are you here?" her mother said.

The girl arranged her veil around her head and face and looked at the ruminating cows. "I came by myself."

"You walked by yourself in the dead of night? Who was with you?"

She continued staring straight at the animals and refused to answer.

Tej fixed her with a fierce glare. "Are you crazy? Don't you know what people will say about us? If I could kill you, I would."

The fugitive maintained a stubborn silence.

"Lock her up without any food. Let her starve until the husband's family comes to fetch her," the younger man said.

Umda Bai turned to face her brothers. "You can starve me to death, but I will never return to my in-laws' house. They beat me, work me like a slave, nor do they give me enough to eat. I will never go back to them. You may as well kill me here and now."

Dark welts showed on her bare arms, and with eyes that were now dry, she looked at her brothers. She had a delicate nose, pink lips and a complexion like a *champa* flower in full bloom. In the light of dawn, her beauty shone like the glowing wick of a candle.

Hearing a shout, her brothers turned on their heels and left the shed. The mother, both dismayed and annoyed, moved towards the door. The eldest wife stole a furtive glance at the bruised face of her sister-in-law who sat in mute anger, and looked away and began cleaning the cowshed.

Umda Bai was tired; she had walked for two nights not daring to walk by day, lest her in-laws send a search party out for her. She had had no food or water, but she felt no hunger, only an immense weariness and lassitude. She sank back on the earthen floor and collapsed into a dreamless sleep while the cows and their calves gave joyful snorts for they had recognized her.

The male siblings stepped outside and saw a farmer sporting a curling moustache, wearing a dirty turban and a coarse tunic and dhoti. He carried a large walking stick.

The two men stared at their visitor. "How are you, Jamunalal-ji? Is everything all right? Why are you here so early?"

"Yes, everything is fine, but we cannot find my brother's wife. Has she come here?"

"Yes."

Jamunalal Singh scowled. "She left our house two nights ago, and we scoured our village as well as the neighboring towns for the last couple of days. Well, she can stay here then, we will not take her back. We will arrange another marriage for my brother."

"No, no, please sit down. Don't be angry with my sister. She is, after all, very young. My grandfather spoiled her rather, and turned her head by calling her a fairy princess because she was so pretty. We will make her see sense and insist that she returns to your family," the second sibling said.

The mother came forward. "I simply don't know what to do with her. She has astonishing courage for a mere girl. She walked all by herself during the night and is far too independent. Please do take her back and if need be, beat her into submission."

The visitor's face reddened with anger and he twirled his moustache. "We have tried beating her black and blue, but to no avail. She is far too stubborn and listens to no one. She is very beautiful and that is why we arranged my brother's marriage with your daughter, but her looks have caused us more problems than we bargained for. Umda Bai attracts far too much attention and it is difficult for us farming folk to maintain strict *purdah* rules at all times. Our women have to draw water from the well, do assorted work in the fields, and in spite of being told to keep herself to herself, she secretly meets and gossips with other girls. Not only that, when men's eyes stray in her direction, she preens. We cannot keep this kind of person as a bride for my brother. Our family will become the laughing-stock of the entire village."

The old woman clasped her hands together. "Please take her back and whip her into submission. She is sure to come to her senses."

The second brother sped indoors and began preparing a *hookah* pipe for their visitor. The three men sat and smoked in a silence that was almost convivial in the face of female intransigence. The mother went to the kitchen to prepare snacks as her daughter's in-laws must be fed, flattered and pleased at all times.

The vegetable fritters were delicious and in the mellow sunshine, the smoke from the pipe curled round Jamunalal's face enveloping him in a warm haze.

He smiled. "Something perhaps could be done to bring the girl to her senses. Someone in my village once mentioned it to me."

"What is it?"

"In days gone by, headstrong women, even if they were married, were sometimes sent over to the palaces to work as maids. Inside the harem, they were worked to the bone and barred from any male contact. Mind you, in that hierarchy they were the lowliest of the low and performed the most menial of chores. After a few years, when their relatives came to claim them, only then were they allowed to leave the royal grounds. By that time all stubbornness would vanish and a creature of utmost docility would emerge."

The mother and her sons listened in rapt silence.

"Do they take just any village girl?" they asked.

"No, one has to know someone among the servants. Perhaps, I can make inquiries through the local grapevine."

"How long will they keep her there?" the old woman asked.

"I really don't know."

Tej stroked the stubble on his chin with his forefinger. "What does Umda's husband, Ganga Singh, have to say about this?"

"My father and mother both support the idea; I, as Ganga's eldest brother, also agree. Why do we need to ask his permission?" Jamunalal's eyes raked the three faces before him, and he tossed back his head. No family business was ever transacted without his concurrence; indeed, the marriages of his brothers and sisters had required the stamp of approval by the family elders.

The mother clutched at her shawl and her two sons gasped.

In the rose-blushed dawn, the cows lowed in their byre, but Umda Bai, overwhelmed with fatigue, lay dead to the world. It was early afternoon when she awoke and saw that the door was ajar with the sunlight streaming in. She walked over to the kitchen and saw her mother up to her elbows in wheat flour.

The old woman looked at her bedraggled daughter, but continued kneading in silence; within moments, she brought out some fresh chapati and a bowl of cooked vegetables. The girl began her meal, tearing off pieces of the round flat bread and stuffing them into her mouth.

"Your brother-in-law came earlier today," the mother said.

The teenager jumped up and shuddered. The bread dropped from her hand. "I am not going back there, I will run away."

The matriarch's demeanor was placid. "All right, don't go back."

Startled, the girl stared at her mother and then sat down again to her meal. Later that evening, a puzzled Umda Bai learned from her sister-in-law that for the next few months or so, she was to go and work in the palace as a maid. Her in-laws had all agreed, and her own family too, had consented. Astonished, the young woman's thoughts flew towards the future, but not to any menial chores that would be her lot. The opulence and luxury of royal living was beyond the confines of her imagination; mud walls, flimsy bamboo doors and home-spun cotton skirts were all she had known. Brick walls, a well-stocked kitchen, a large grinding stone, bright clothes and jewels captured her imagination, and that was as far as she dared to dream.

The day soon arrived for Umda Bai's trip. The mother slathered her child's unkempt hair with clarified butter, combed it and patted in melted wax to make it shiny, and coiled the tresses into a high top-knot. The prospective maid was dressed in a clean skirt and blouse, and as much jewelry as the family could muster; a long scarf of soft cotton veiled her head and face. With her mother, Tej and Jamunalal, she left her dwelling and began her trek to the capital. Unaware of the girl's daydreams, the family had been agreeably surprised at her ready acquiescence.

The journey took several days and they passed a number of tiny hamlets where they stayed with kinfolk. Upon arrival in the city, they called on personal acquaintances and friends of relatives who were known to the guards and servants, until finally they were permitted entry into the palace. Their turbans dust-begrimed, Umda Bai's brother and brother-in-law, the one still carrying his huge stick, were told to wait by the seventh and outermost gate whilst the women went inside. A royal eunuch escorted the two ladies to the inner apartments to meet the senior-most attendant to the queen. The teenager's dirt-caked feet could be seen beneath her long skirt that was worn a little high like all village girls. The daughter and mother joined their henna-patterned palms in greeting and bowed their heads.

"Why are you veiling yourselves in the harem? Come with me to see Her Majesty. Let us see if you meet with her approval," the aide said.

She led them to Rani Tomarji's villa in the palace grounds and at the doorway to the royal apartments, she told them to wait while she alone entered and described stories, duly embellished, of the girl's unladylike behavior.

She returned to them and beckoned to Umda Bai. "Now, lift your head and watch me carefully. This is how you should greet her."

The young woman removed her veil and bowed low before the august lady and stepped back, head still lowered. The rani lay on her cushioned divan, surrounded by her ladies-in-waiting on the marble terrace. It was early evening and the light from the oil lamps fell on the floral murals on the walls, and it also fell on the face of the visitor. The queen's eyes widened as she looked at Umda Bai, astonished at the delicacy of feature in a mere farm girl.

The newcomer, unaware of the stir she had caused, gazed in child-like wonder at the luxurious apartments, at the bejeweled queen and her silk-clad ladies, then bent her head and eyed the royal assembly through her lashes.

Years passed. One day, Ganga Singh, Umda Bai's husband, arrived at his in-laws' home and sought out the head of the family.

"I have come to take my wife back. Perhaps you and your mother will accompany me to the palace. By now, doubtless, she has seen the error of her ways, and will be able to keep house for me," he said.

Tej remained silent. He had heard whispers of his sister's dazzling rise to fame in the royal harem; the beguiled king had bestowed on her many favors. If he had been secretly pleased at her success, today he stood ashamed and mortified before the simple farmer. He had never bothered to request his sibling's return in order to hand her back to the in-laws; although in truth, it could be said that they had never asked for Umda Bai either.

Tej frowned. "Why didn't you come earlier?"

Ganga flushed and tugged at his earlobe. "My mother died, then so did my father, my older brother fell seriously ill and we suffered crop failure on our farm. I thought that with all our problems, she might run away again. Meanwhile, I took a job in the army and did not get leave until now."

His mother-in-law gave him a fond glance and thought what a delightful pair her daughter and this well-built man made and silently prayed for a covey of grandchildren.

"Come, let us go and bring her back from the palace," she said.

So, along with the old woman, the two farmers set off on the long journey.

At the entrance, the men were stopped once again by the sentries at the outermost gate, and only the mother was allowed to proceed inside.

"Whom do you wish to see?" asked a royal guard.

"I have come to take Umda home," the woman said.

"We don't have anybody by that name here. You say that she works as a maid for a queen? Which queen?"

The visitor's voice did not rise above a whisper.

"Rani Tomarji."

"All right, we will send word to her ladies. Wait here." Jerking his head, the man called out to one of his underlings. "Go notify the eunuchs."

The woman sat among the many supplicants for royal largesse in a walled courtyard, shielded from men and waited her turn.

Upon receiving the news, the chief eunuch went inside the harem and asked for the queen's principal lady-in-waiting. She emerged with an air of weary disdain from the interior apartments, a handful of her personal maids in tow.

"Who are you? Whom do you wish to see?" she said.

The male guardian stepped forward. "You are Umda's mother and you have come to take her home? Who is Umda?"

The old woman, her head still bent, described the girl in detail.

The man threw back his head and his lips quivered. "Oh, don't you know? There is no Umda Bai here anymore. His Majesty has given her a new name and title, Sumeru Rai, Pardayet.

"She is your daughter and you want to see her? What? Her husband has come to take her home you say? She is not your child any longer, she is almost like a queen now. Don't you ever dare say that she has a spouse; if you do, all of you will be clapped in jail. Return to your village, my good woman, and don't come back."

The palace functionaries shook with laughter as the guards escorted the woman out of the gates to her waiting son and son-in-law.

Shortly afterwards, Umda Bai's family heard that she had been visited by the Goddess Ganga Devi. One full moon night, the concubine sat in the corner of the rooftop garden by the marble fountains and quivered in divine ecstasy. Sprays of water had soaked her limbs, and her clothes clung to her body. A eunuch informed the king that the Goddess had appeared before Sumeru Rai; the ruler, his brain befuddled with wine, saw the drenched figure of his mistress who told him that she was no longer a mere courtesan, but an emissary of a higher power. Bemused, he embraced her and readily acquiesced to all her wishes. From that moment onwards, during full moon or at any astrologically auspicious moment, she sought audience with the king, claiming occult powers. Affairs of state and bestowal of favors on palace personnel became part of pillow talk. The sovereign ceased to view her as another talented dancer, but rather a voluptuous harbinger of news from the world beyond and, fearful of inculcating divine wrath he followed her advice, most of which dwelt on affairs of the harem. If any of the concubines the king dallied with dared challenge the courtesan, she was identified by Sumeru as evil and dangerous and sent to the dungeons. If the woman was beautiful, death by slow poison was likely to be her eventual fate.

Claiming that she was ordained by God to protect his kingdom, she held her lover in thrall. Exulting in her power, she ventured advice on matters of state, at times overruling the counsel he received from his able ministers. Whispers arose that she was the force behind the throne, rather like the legendary Noor Jahan; the courtiers feared the concubine and the palace minions ascribed to her supernatural abilities in divining the future. The news spread further and there came a time when the village folk viewed her as second only to their ruler.

The king, already old, grew feeble and died on a winter's night. The course of life in the harem continued; the new maharaja had little use for his father's aging mistress or her oracular prophesies. Overnight, she was dethroned from her deity-like status, and those who had been deprived of privileges or otherwise punished by their former ruler took a vengeful delight in her downfall. Those who had believed in her mystic powers were disillusioned.

The queens underwent a change of status from being consorts to queen mothers, but remained royalty nonetheless; the favorites of the harem found their powers vanish. The new occupant of the throne had no use for their feminine wiles or their coquettish ways and spent his leisure hours in the embraces of a new troupe of younger, nubile concubines. Sumeru, to her dismay, found that no longer did the servants scurry like frightened rabbits at her slightest frown, nor did they hang from her lips for prophetic pronouncements. Her apartment remained elegantly furnished and her privileges continued uninterrupted, but she joined the ranks of former courtesans who lived out their days in luxurious obscurity. Still beautiful and ambitious, with an incisive intelligence, she continued holding court to an ever-dwindling coterie of admirers.

One afternoon, amidst desultory conversation with some of her attendants, Sumeru heard the story of her mother's arrival at the palace gates and of her summary departure.

"Why didn't you let her in? Why did no one inform me?"

"She had on such dirty clothes, and spoke in such a rustic tongue, we didn't believe that this village woman could be your mother, Bai Saheb," a maid said. No longer awed by the courtesan, she curled her lips. "The crone even said that she had come with her son and son-in-law. They wanted to see you, and not only that, they wanted to take you home with them."

The dethroned concubine turned her coiffed head, pursed her lips and glared at the servant; why, while the former king was alive, all the domestic help fought with each other for the privilege of waiting on her hand and foot.

The maid giggled and gave a side-long glance at her mistress. "The chief eunuch and the principal lady-in-waiting couldn't stop laughing. They told her, 'Flee the city right away. Your daughter is like a queen. If you ever again refer to that oaf as her husband, you will all be clapped in jail.'"

Sumeru remained silent. Memories of a half-forgotten childhood flooded through her mind. Was her mother still alive? Her brothers no doubt were. Oh, the freedom of her village days. The apartment with its carved furniture and silk quilts seemed oppressive; the marble filigree work on the windows through which the blue of the heavens could be seen, prison bars. A desperate longing for the vast outdoors, the scrub grass, sunbaked dirt roads and the muddy path to the well coursed through her veins. Although still beautiful, her power had vanished with the death of the king, and she wallowed in nostalgia.

The maid's voice was thin and obsequious. "They came again the other day as well."

The lady feigned nonchalance, her pride far outweighed by her curiosity. "Who came, my mother? Why did she come again?"

The domestic suppressed a smile. "She arrived with her son and son-in-law. There was also a little boy with them. They are staying somewhere in the city."

"Who was the boy?"

"He was the son-in-law's child. The men had come to look for jobs as sentries or guards at the palace, I heard the eunuchs say. Well, it won't be of any use for them to approach you, as your word doesn't carry much weight anymore."

Sumeru knitted her brows and clenched her teeth. The impudence of these maids, they would never have dared speak to her in that manner earlier. She ignored the gossipmonger and stared straight ahead.

"I heard that the boy was very good-looking. He is about twelve or thirteen years old, and carried an enormous sword on his lap as he sat between his father and uncle. He'll grow up to be a fine young man." The maid paused and affected a puzzled air. "Would that be your son, Bai Saheb?"

The former concubine wrapped her scattered shreds of dignity tightly around herself. "Go and tell the servants to sprinkle more water on the *khus khus* screens, it is very hot and stuffy in here. Also, tell them to pull the fans harder; I am going to lie down."

The maids alluded to the youth from time to time, but Sumeru ignored them. Homesickness gnawed at her; she thought of her own family and she also wondered when her husband had remarried, and to whom. The woman must be beautiful to have produced such an offspring. Sometimes, when she promenaded on the rooftop garden and gazed up at the vast expanse of blue brushed by white goose feathers of clouds, she longed for her mother and village home. She wondered too, about her co-wife and whether she was prettier than she, and of the son.

During the heavy drowse of the afternoons, while a maid massaged her feet and another combed her tresses, Sumeru, with seeming reluctance, listened to their murmurs. Town and village gossip combined to form an intoxicating blend and became a regular backdrop to her massages.

One afternoon, she drew aside a trustworthy servant. "Why don't we slip out one day and visit our village?"

The maid stared at her mistress aghast. Was the Bai Saheb out of her mind? "We do not have permission. I have never heard of anyone stepping outside the harem."

Sumeru remained silent and a few days went by. Once again, she summoned her confidante. "Why don't we slip out with the people who scrub our floors? We can dress in shabby garments and return to the palace after a few days."

The maid's jaw dropped. A faint longing for freedom stirred inside her brain.

"What if I took all my jewelry? Why don't we both run away? What joy is there for us being imprisoned here?" Sumeru said.

The concubine owned a treasure chest of jewels. Pearls, rubies and diamonds had been given to her by the old maharaja; hope and longing rising unbidden in her breast, the servant gloated over the unseen gems. Desultory talk gave way to determined planning; hope replaced fear. They planned their flight in hasty, secret confabulations. They decided to enlist the aid of two trusted menials to serve as lookouts.

The evening of their planned departure came.

"I will go on ahead, and you follow me," Sumeru said.

The two women looked at each other, their eyes alight with triumph, though traces of fear lurked in their depths. The courtesan sat on the bed, bent down and undid her silver anklets and cast them aside. She shed her silk blouse and skirt, wrapped herself in tattered clothes borrowed from a maid, strung all her necklaces together and wound them around her waist, secreted the rest of the jewelry in the folds of her shawl and stepped out of the room.

Her maid, in similar garb, crept out a while later.

Sumeru walked along the corridors of the palace. It was a virtual labyrinth. She tried to recall her entry into the abode many years ago; as a teenager she had come with her mother, but she had been so swathed in veils that she may as well have been blindfolded. From that day onwards, the harem had been her home. She glanced back and saw her servant creeping in stealthy footsteps behind her. They moved forward but their gait was uncertain and their pace, slow.

A stream of cold air blew in and ruffled their head coverings. In the distance they heard a cough and the sound of a man clearing his throat. The concubine's pace quickened and she grabbed her companion's hand; though almost blinded by their veils, they were near the entrance.

"Halt. Who goes there?" A male voice sounded in the darkness.

Footsteps approached, but the two women ignored them.

Three men came running and barred their way.

A guard, thick staff in hand, stood before the ladies. "The washroom cleaners have already left for the day; a while back, in fact. Why are you wandering around in the courtyard?" He turned his head towards one of his assistants. "Go, get the eunuchs."

A short while later, Sumeru returned to her apartment on the arm of the chief eunuch; her maid too was escorted by one of the many men who patrolled the harem. That night, by command of the dowager maharani, the concubine's jewelry became Crown property. The maids gathered around her and clawed off her necklaces, bangles and nose rings.

She was relegated to a windowless room and her bed became a threadbare mat on the floor. In due course, she learned from the servants that the widowed queen planned on building a temple within the palace grounds to honor her husband, the late maharaja, from the sale of Sumeru's jewels.

Despondent in her spartan surroundings, she took cheer in that bit of news. Her name too, would be etched on the walls; she had after all, been a source of great solace to the king in his declining years and besides, the place was being built with her gems. Doubtless, once the structure was finished, she would be carried there in a palanquin.

Upon completion, by permission of the dowager maharani, the queens, concubines and even the maids visited the edifice, but there were no summons for Sumeru. She sank back in her room vacant-eyed and listless, and scraps of memory of her village and former husband coalesced into a jumbled mass, causing her at times to laugh in sheer abandon, and at times to weep.

Bereft of her treasures and unable to bribe, but using remnants of her powerful personality, she coaxed forbidden wine from the maids. Reality blurred into fantasy in her alcohol-addled brain and she dreamed of the temple as a tribute to herself and her royal lover.

The Mistress Wife
Shethanijee

The awaited invitation embossed with the royal seal arrived at last. She tore open the envelope in feverish haste and pored over the details. Rani Chandavatji, the third queen, had requested the pleasure of her company to a dance performance to be held at the palace. When Shethanijee was young, she had attended these festivities with her family, but, for some reason, the summonses had ceased. Throughout her childhood, during the afternoons when time hung heavy, her grandmother would unlock a treasure chest of tales and weave stories replete with castles and kings, and queens and concubines, to an audience of enthralled children.

The fabled abode loomed large over the kingdom and cast both its shadow and its spell over the inhabitants. During her pre-teen years, she would gaze as though in a dream at the edifice from her rooftop, impatient for the overtures to resume. When the maharaja and his sons rode on their elephants, the gilded howdahs on the pachyderms' backs swaying gently, she, along with her brothers, sisters and cousins, would race to the veranda to catch a glimpse of the procession in the distance.

Holding the card in one hand, she waltzed to the wardrobe to select clothing fit for a royal visit. Long skirts, *choli* blouses and veils in yellow, green and cerulean, reflecting the seasons glimmered inside the armoire. Which outfit would catch the maharaja's eye she wondered, as the silks and muslins rippled through her fingers. The crown prince of her childhood was now the king.

She heard her husband downstairs call out to a servant. The visions of regal opulence vanished to be replaced by the visage of her spouse; he was a plain man, some might call him ugly. Short, hunched, more dwarf than person, Shyamnath Sheth was the only son of a wealthy businessman whose property holdings alone might put some hereditary landlords, the zamindars, to shame. She had been given in marriage to him when she was barely in her teens, it had been an advantageous match, her parents said, that of all the moneyed families, his had been the most prosperous. Besides, what he lacked in looks was more than made up for by his financial acumen. Unkind people called him an impotent midget, but he had a son and daughter by her to prove otherwise.

Shethanijee opened all the jewelry boxes and drew out diamond-studded tiaras, pearl necklaces, gold chokers, earrings, bangles, ruby rings and emerald bracelets and laid them out on silver platters.

The woman's face stared back from one of the yet empty gleaming trays and she lifted it up and continued gazing at the reflection, an absent frown on her brow. She was still attractive, but would her looks rival those of the king's concubines? Beauties from the entire kingdom were culled and brought to the palace, indeed many a family sold or gave their daughters to swell the harem ranks. Would the maharaja even glance in her direction? If only the invitation had arrived a few years earlier.

She scrutinized her countenance again with care—were there any crow's-feet? Her hair was no longer as luxuriant as in her youth, but in her expressive eyes lay hidden depths of emotion. The summons had come too late; she twirled the round tray and her mouth drooped. The lady gave a start when she realized that she was not glancing at a real mirror and replaced it on the table with a thud, but a while later picked it up and gazed at herself again. The sun's last rays through the window bathed the room in a rosy glow and she smiled. Her features were still charming, with arched eyebrows, curling lashes, a full-lipped mouth, all framed by a mass of dark hair.

Her husband entered the room in silence and stood nearby. He was very proud of his beautiful, witty wife and her exquisite taste in clothes.

"Going through your jewelry, I see. Do you want me to order some more for you?" he said.

Seeing her spouse's reflection, she lowered the make-believe mirror.

"No, I don't want any new necklaces, I will choose from these. What I would really like to wear are things that would appear unusual even to the queens."

Mr Sheth seated himself, while their two children, a stripling of a boy and a girl in her mid-teens, entered the room.

"I myself have never seen all our family baubles, although I do recall that there are a few stunning pieces," the man said. "My mother once heard my father mention multiple strands of pearls as well as a sapphire bracelet that my grandmother received as part of her dowry. She was the daughter of a prosperous businessman in Kathiawar. They should be here somewhere as she wore them on a palace visit."

"But that will be old stuff, nothing new to people there," the youngsters said.

Their mother laughed. "Yes, they are antique pieces no doubt, but those who have seen them before are long dead."

Both husband and wife sifted through the many boxes that lay strewn on the carpet. The woman opened marble containers inlaid with jade and carnelian, as well as carved wooden chests, and pulled out necklace after necklace. Mr Sheth squinted at each one with a professional air before setting it aside.

His wife extracted some pearls. "Is this the one?"

The piece dangled from her fingers, rivulets of glistening milk-white globules. The outsized gold locket set with rubies and diamonds shot back fire in the rays of the setting sun.

Mr Sheth's eyes widened and his jaw dropped. "Yes, that must be it. The local jewelers often send us their wares for approval, but I have never set eyes on anything like it."

The children stroked the pearls. Their mother selected that gem-studded creation, a hundred-year-old sapphire bracelet still in its original setting, gold chokers, some bangles and a jewel-encrusted *tikli* for her hair.

She began daydreaming about her impending visit. The concubines no doubt were good-looking, but were the queens attractive as well? She had heard that women remained veiled at all royal festivities, except for the maharani. The beauty of the harem residents was legendary and their clothes too would be gorgeous. She herself would have to cover her head and face, but do it in such a manner so as to be able to peer at the assembled ladies.

Late one evening, the domed wooden carriage pulled by two white oxen and accompanied by an escort of crimson-clad men holding flaming torches, made its way down the street. The conveyance, with heavy curtains cloaking its sides from top to bottom to shield women from public gaze, came to a halt by Shethanijee's house. She had been busy with her toilette since mid-afternoon, and when the coach came, she climbed in with a handful of her maids. Once they reached the palace gates, they were whisked through a honeycomb of deserted passages by the eunuch who was the sole bridge between the outside and the mysterious world within.

The king and his queens sat at one end of the inner courtyard. Troupes of dancers, some in lime green, others in pinks, mauves and blues, glided in and performed their routines to the tinkle of hand cymbals and haunting music. Enchanted, the merchant's wife drank in all the details through a tiny gap in her veil.

The show ended and the chief eunuch brought each guest, in order of her social rank, before the royal personages. The newcomer's turn arrived and she was escorted to their majesties and, at a signal from the guide, she bowed and raised palm to forehead, then extended her hand and presented the king the customary *nazar*, the token gift of a coin wrapped in spotless white linen. The ruler reached out and brushed his hand against her fingertips. His eyes swept over her figure as she bent over, the pearl necklace hanging low over the form-fitting blouse, the sapphire bracelet winking in the lamplight. She proceeded toward the maharani and half knelt; the queen, a frown creasing her brow, accepted the woman's homage.

No, Shethanijee was not mistaken; time had not yet passed her by. She might no longer have been in her first youth, but she was still attractive nonetheless; her lissome grace had been replaced by a voluptuous maturity, the virgin blushes, by a deceptive coyness. Kohl-rimmed eyes downcast, face hidden by a chiffon veil, she returned to her seat demure and deferential.

Invitations began pouring in from the palace. The junior queens invited her to their private festivities as she always brought tidbits of salacious gossip from town, until the day came when the maharani herself sought her presence at a soirée. The ranis, who had never set foot beyond the palace walls, were fascinated by this woman from the world outside. Her manner was pleasing, and gifts more so. Garlands of fresh marigolds, still moist with dew, and bunches of jasmine were the frequent offerings she made to the queens and, on occasion, she would present them with a choker or bracelet fashioned by her personal jeweler. Such pieces had a unique and distinctive charm, a change from the ornate items worn by royalty.

During the afternoons, when the queens and their ladies-in-waiting played cards or chess, Shethanijee joined in and very wisely lost every game. If the king's consorts complained of poor health, she sat by their bedsides and soothed their fevered brows. Her largesse was not confined to those born to the purple; for their attendants and the many dancers she brought homemade pickles, spiced dumplings, vegetable fritters and other edibles. She wore a new outfit for every visit and her long silk skirts, blouses and veils shimmered in rich colors and were well matched. During the evenings, she regaled her extended family with tales from the august abode, indeed, at home she was not the supplicant, but held court like their majesties.

The king's curiosity, too, was piqued. He had heard some of Shethanijee's stories through his queens and courtesans. The joys and sorrows of his subjects as well as the daily trials and tribulations of the common folk were news to him, so he would ask for more through his wives.

To the ladies of the harem, family life and the world outside were foreign. Shethanijee's chatter about children, husbands, wives, shopping, bazaars and mundane domestic details evoked a vista of a forbidden world and in each woman, queen or concubine sprang an unbidden longing. Curious, but with a sneaking sense of envy, they panted for more.

With kohl-rimmed eyes alight behind the filmy veil, the visitor poured forth a wealth of heavily embellished tales. Some were pure inventions, yet others bore some semblance to the truth, but all were recounted in a melodious voice. Her whole body quivered as she spoke, her mehndi-painted hands fluttered as she gestured and her earrings swung to and fro. At times she would give a coy toss of her head and with one hand tug at the veil—just enough to ruffle the brocaded edge.

The day arrived when the ruler himself, keen on meeting the person who had caused such a sensation, summoned her to his presence.

Before the king, she dropped her veil. She remained a frequent visitor to the palace, but now primarily, to his apartments.

The maharani and the lesser queens, furious at this presumptuous woman, vented their anger at Rani Chandavatji. She had, after all, invited this creature into their midst. Their marriages were political alliances and none could claim to be the maharaja's darling, but nevertheless there was a nuanced hierarchy in the royal residence.

The third rani, incensed by Shethanijee's impudence, sent word through a messenger to the interloper's husband. He merely laughed. His wife was mistress to the maharaja—what a great source of pride, his own business would flourish even further, now that she had the royal ear.

The concubines were no less outraged; the monarch had barely a glance for them these days, so taken was he with the newcomer.

One afternoon, at the third queen's villa, a young dancer approached Shethanijee. "You have such lustrous hair. May I show you a new type of coiffure?"

The lady, pleased at the compliment, complied. The teenager removed the older woman's filmy scarf. With great care she took off the gold *tikli* with the gleaming medallion from her head, then unclasped the earrings, uncoiled her tresses and removed the brocade ribbons. Something else shone too, as the hair hung loose—a few strands of pure silver.

The girl giggled. "Oh, Shethanijee, you are going grey!"

The guest grabbed the *tikli*, put on the earrings and quickly covered her head with the veil, the braids undone. In the sunlit room, her glance fell on her reflection in the mirror on the wall—the lines beneath the eyes seemed as pronounced as the furrows in the barley fields after a downpour.

Rani Chandavatji, reclining on a silver bedstead overlooking the inner courtyard, saw the tableau; while the maids wielded peacock-feather fans and a masseuse tended to her ankles, a faint smile appeared on her lips and then vanished in an instant. Some of the attendants gave derisive smiles, others sniggered, and all those who had been discomfited by the visitor's brazen attempts to usurp the coveted position of the king's favorite could scarcely contain their glee.

Later that day, Shethanijee wept in mortification before the maharaja. The story tumbled out: how she had been tricked into loosening her hair and how the women had tittered, and the tales, all duly embellished, she poured into his sympathetic ear. She was careful to omit mention of the chalky streaks, but rather gave him to understand that the mirth was occasioned by her disheveled appearance deliberately caused by a danseuse in the third queen's entourage.

The tears were not shed in vain. Over a period of time, the privileges accorded to women of status ended for Rani Chandavatji—no longer did the maids arrive with a tray laden with betel leaf wraps from the royal refectory for her ladies-in-waiting to munch on during the afternoons. Offended, she repudiated all special benefits.

The scorching heat of the Rajasthan summers gave way to autumnal mists, presaging a crisp winter. The third rani caught a severe chill and, as she lay supine with a raging fever, her co-wives visited her from time to time.

The sovereign also received news of his spouse's sudden illness. The chief eunuch was dispatched to her bedchamber with a tray-load of medicine as well as unguents for her aching limbs.

One day, the man arrived at her door, his manner deferential and tone solicitous. "His Majesty has enquired after your health, Your Majesty. The doctor will be coming soon. Do you have any special request or message for His Majesty?"

The queen, still smarting from the maharaja's slights, said, "He is very kind. I have no desires that he can possibly meet. Just tell him to remain ever hostage to that upstart, that would-be concubine."

Within a few weeks, she succumbed to her malady. Ill health plagued many women in the harem, so her death caused no surprise. A grand funeral was held in her honor and there was a great public ritual display of sorrowing, but a while later the palace returned to its well-worn routines.

The ruler had no dearth of women to flatter, charm and console him as the need arose, so the monarch's wife was soon a mere memory, but her parting taunt had hurt his pride, and continued to rankle. The precise details of his mistress's hair-loosening incident also came to his ears through his concubines, who themselves had heard the story from the maids. The number of snowy strands in the lady's hair had, moreover, multiplied tenfold in the local gossip.

One evening, as Shethanijee came for her daily audience with the king, he kept gazing at her face for long periods of time in silence. During their amorous dalliances she had always managed to keep well-coiffed, even when the gold *tikli* and hairpins ran askew. She was a breath of fresh air in the gilded dwelling. Her musical talent might not compare to that of his courtesans who were well-versed in the arts, but her tart wit and news about town were enlivening. She was a born conversationalist and knew how to please her royal lover. That night, however, the easy chatter and glib flattery bored him; the novelty of having a townswoman visit him was beginning to pall.

He interrupted and faced his companion with engaging curiosity. "You have children, don't you?" Without waiting for a reply, he reached out and twisted a strand of her long curls around his forefinger. "How old are they? I have heard that you have a daughter. Is she as attractive as you? Why don't you bring her along one day?"

He gazed at his mistress's heart-shaped face framed by her sleek tresses, and in him stirred the longings for a more youthful, nubile Shethanijee with gleaming limbs and clouds of dark hair.

The lady started. Her smile vanished. Protective maternal eyes glittered at the maharaja through a courtesan's veil. Her coquetry disappeared and lower lip quivered.

The silence was broken by a trembling voice. "But my girl is very young, besides, she just got married."

"Young? How old is she?"

The woman's voice was muffled and she looked down at the floor. "She turned fifteen last year."

Her paramour's tone was amused, his manner teasing. "Fifteen or sixteen! Oh, then it is true what Rani Chandavatji's ladies said, that you are getting on in years."

The mother remained wordless and her head drooped. It was at her behest that the queen's privileges were taken away. Face flaming, she bore her lover's snubs in silence.

"On your next visit, please bring your daughter along. I will order the carriage for you," he said.

The royal conveyance arrived at Shethanijee's doorstep a few days later and returned to the palace, but with only one passenger, not two. The eunuch guided her to the maharaja's villa where a dance performance was in progress. She bowed low before the king and begged forgiveness for her lone visit and explained that the teenager's in-laws had taken the girl to meet relatives in Bikaner, a town some distance away. Jewelry glittering, ashen-faced behind her veil, she gazed at him in anguish.

The sovereign, enjoying the pirouettes of his courtesans, barely glanced at her. When evening ended, a servant escorted the visitor back to the waiting carriage and informed the lady that the monarch had commanded her to visit him every night.

A separate suite was set aside in the women's quarters. Daily, she sat awaiting her lover but his visits were infrequent, and she sat in unaccustomed solitude most of the time. A few days later, word came through an emissary that she was to make her home there for a while.

Shethanijee's new residence was a room furnished with an ivory-inlaid bedstead and enameled brass tables. Her youthful liveliness had vanished, her eyes were bereft of their sparkle, and the tiny wrinkles by the mouth, more pronounced. No longer could she regale the cloistered inhabitants with gossip from town; she was a prisoner like the concubines. Her hand trembled when applying *kohl* around the eyes and her hair had lost its sheen.

The ladies in the harem were stunned by the metamorphosis. She, who had been a much feted guest, an object of both admiration and envy, now shared the fate of a discarded mistress. Some whispered amongst themselves that the woman was unwell and needed a doctor.

One day the eunuch stopped by. "How are you, Madam?"

"Please ask His Majesty to allow me to go home. I am not feeling well," she said.

He left the room and returned some time later with a tray of tonics. "The maharaja has sent these. The doctor has been summoned, so please convalesce here. You can return once you are better."

She squinted at the cups. "What kind of medicine is that?"

The man remained silent. The woman had been guilty of *lèse-majesté*. Why, so many people in the kingdom were eager to offer their daughters to the palace. He stroked his upper lip. "I don't know."

For almost a month, Shethanijee languished in that room. Her hair loose and lank, and face robbed of its habitual gaiety, she stared unseeingly at the distant hills visible from the window. Questions arose in her mind, but she stilled them with difficulty. Her self-assurance had vanished and the light-hearted banter with the king was now a mere memory.

One evening, when the eunuch arrived to ply her with the daily potions, she turned and faced him. "When can I leave?

How long do I have to swallow this stuff? It doesn't make me any better."

The attendant eyed her in silence. "You must drink it, as it is His Majesty's command. He only wants you to get well before he orders the carriage to send you home. This herbal extract is used for the fevers and chills that sicken so many of our women." He paused for a moment. "Why, Rani Chandavatji used to take this medication."

Shethanijee swung around and stared at him, her eyes widening. She sat in silence while the many tales of the harem she had heard as a child crowded into her brain. She tried to speak, but no sound emerged from her throat.

The aide, motioning the maids to remain quiet, turned and left.

The royal guest passed a sleepless night, drenched in a cold sweat. The golden moon, large and full, bathed the rooftop gardens in an ethereal glow, but she saw only monstrous shapes and deep shadows.

Next morning, the doctor made his visit. He sat on one side of the curtain hung to protect feminine modesty while the maids by Shethanijee's bed answered his questions and received instructions.

Suitable invalid fare must be given, heard the sick lady who lay weak with fatigue. She almost cried out to the physician for he was the only link to the outside world, but she could barely lift her head from the pillow. Would he listen, or would he dismiss her fears as the imaginings of an overwrought patient? The women who attended her also tended to the draperies and the callers without. Could she trust any of the servants and plead an audience with the monarch and beg to be sent home? Were there any allies within these luxurious walled precincts? In her heyday as a much-awaited visitor, she had spawned enemies, not friends.

Midday, the maids brought vegetable broth ideal for an invalid's palate, but the aroma merely sickened her, and the bowl remained untouched. Tears streamed down her cheeks as she lay outstretched on the divan; she longed for her misshapen husband's tenderness and the children's laughter.

When evening arrived, female servants lit the oil lamps in the room and the eunuch entered with a tray of herbal tonics.

Shethanijee half rose and clutched at the pillows. "That medicine tastes bitter. I am not going to take it anymore."

The man averted his face and fiddled with the items on the bedside table. "You will get better, my lady. Drink it up. It has been sent to you by His Majesty."

The attendants crowded in. One lifted her up and another pressed the glass to her lips. Afterwards, the male aide left the room with the empty container. The patient sank back against the cushions and the women cooled her with long-handled fans.

Confused thoughts screamed inside the prisoner's brain. It had been her ardent wish since childhood to be invited to the palace and here she lay, at the mercy of the man she had sought to enslave. Was she being punished for not procuring her offspring to whet the maharaja's appetite? Would she be released if she did? The teen lived with her in-laws' extended family; besides, it was better that she alone should suffer. The king had a surfeit of women; was he being merely punitive at her defiance? Or perhaps this was mere royal caprice, and he might release her at some future date? He was surrounded by beauties adept in the art of coquetry...what if he forgot altogether?

The shadows lengthened on the rooftop gardens and the myna birds took wing.

The Princess Baby
Beti ka Bap

A fig tree towered over the well, which was about seven feet around, the water barely visible in its inky depths. The oxen, with thick ropes slung around their necks, moved in rhythmic unison down the slope. A taut goat-skin bag appeared over the rim of the well and tipped over, pouring streams of water into the many tiny canals and gullies crisscrossing the fields. The man tending the beasts hummed an age-old tune under his breath as the bag wheezed up the moist inner wall.

"Oh, may the waters fill and flow," sang a woman as she poured the liquid into her earthenware pots. Balancing all three containers one on top of the other on her head, her long scarf falling past her shoulders, she navigated her way along the muddy path and walked with a swinging gait back to her home.

The farmers, their hands busy maneuvering the ropes around their animals' necks, exchanged pleasantries but were careful to keep a fair distance away from the women. A couple of village ladies squatted on the ground and scrubbed their pots with dry sand until the vessels, made with a mixture of earth and ground copper, gleamed in the morning sunlight.

A grey-haired woman with two little girls in tow appeared at the scene. The murmurs of conversation ended mid-sentence, the snatches of song stopped abruptly, feminine hands polishing the pitchers paused in mid-air. People turned to stare; this grandmother was rarely seen at the well. Two or three women were standing aside engaged in conversation. A peal of derisive laughter burst forth.

One of the women turned to the visitor. "Have you a new grandson?"

Bhuri Bai frowned. "Why do you ask? You have already visited our house earlier this morning. Is this a joke?"

"When did I ever stop by your house?"

"Why, you were outside our cottage this morning. You said, 'Goodness, another girl, what folly.' I was in another room, but my younger son overheard you and told me all about it later."

The first speaker affected great surprise and cupped her cheek with one hand. "Look at Kushal Singh's mother! I have come to the well straight from home. Her house is on the way so naturally I stopped by, but only for a moment, mind you. When did I have time for all this conversation that she attributes to me?" She tossed her head. "Your younger son Santosh Singh is a liar. And is there any crime in remarking on whether the baby is a boy or a girl?"

The elderly woman's face flushed, but she made no reply.

Meanwhile, all work by the well had ceased. The village women, amazement flitting over their faces, gathered around the two bickering ladies.

"The birth of a child is joyful indeed. So what if it is a daughter, and the sixth one at that? It is no doubt delightful that your family of Rajput descent is so prolific in girls. Why are you so angry at my stating the obvious? Don't you remember your mother taunting my aunt when she had four daughters and no sons?"

Bhuri Bai raised her eyebrows. "When did my mother make fun of your aunt? Stop this lying."

The altercation ran fast and furious. Some years ago, a gossip named Moti Bai had sneered at the woman's aunt saying that Kushal Singh's grandmothers were privately commiserating over the family's misfortune. 'All girls and no boys' was indeed a calamity for a family who claimed ancestral descent from the warrior caste.

The men standing nearby fell silent, discomfited and annoyed at this display of spite. They remained aloof however; some stood apart and chewed tobacco and others drew water from the well while the speaker continued her acerbic banter. The sun rose higher in the heavens casting a haze over the ploughed fields. The old woman, with a sudden start recalling her waiting daughter-in-law and the newborn, grabbed at her two grandchildren.

She strode home seething with anger while her thoughts flew to her sons, the older, Kushal, who was a corporal, and Santosh, who tended the family's acres and was the village headman. Though Kushal's wife had first given birth to a daughter, mercifully their next child had been a boy. Descended as they were from a distant branch of the Rajputs, family honor demanded a son. As for her younger daughter-in-law, she had had nothing but girls. They had all hoped and prayed for a male offspring; six females would lighten their coffers considerably, but to their utter dismay the new baby was a girl. Some of their relatives had sneered and others had offered condolences while disguising their delight. Her sons' in-laws were modest landowners in the neighboring villages, and her boys had commanded substantial dowries. The veiled barbs at the well from Ganeshi Bai, a distant relative by marriage, were more than she could stomach.

Reaching home, she peeped into the room where her daughter-in-law lay sleeping with the baby beside her. The child was a darling; with a petal-soft skin and dimpled arms, her translucent lips slightly parted, it was as though a dew-laden rose had been dropped on the bed.

A girl slipped into the room. "Look Grandma, Mummy has such a pretty doll."

A faint smile softened Bhuri Bai's countenance. "Yes, indeed."

Yes indeed, the newborn was beautiful, thought the old woman. That is why...that is why what? Aloud she called out to her older son's wife. "Have you given the new mother tea or some freshly ground spices stirred in warm water? When did the nurse-midwife say she would come again? Surely she will be back to give the baby and mother their massages?"

The woman pulled at her long scarf, covered her head and answered her mother-in-law.

Bhuri Bai gathered all her grandchildren and took them to the front porch.

"Tell us a story, Grandma!"

Her sons were both out, and the elder daughter-in-law was busy kneading flour for chapati. She gazed at the brood around her and gave a fond glance at her sole grandson who was good-looking, sturdy and a credit to their family. Her eyes slid past him to her granddaughters, their complexions a delicate peach and eyes alight with anticipation. Her fury slowly ebbed; her grandchildren were adorable. Her anger, though, had not entirely melted; her younger son would always be referred to as the 'father of daughters' or *beti ka bap*. She pulled the girls towards her one by one and started combing their hair; as her gnarled but nimble fingers twisted their locks into tight braids, in a reedy monotone she told them stories of far-off days.

The tales rolled off her lips but her thoughts lay elsewhere. People said that times had changed, but had they? Otherwise, how dare Ganeshi Bai insult her in that manner? So what if the baby was beautiful. That evening she told her sons of the insult to their family.

"We need to decide on a course of action," she said.

"What type of action?" Kushal said.

"I'll let you know when I decide. We'll wait until the mother emerges from her confinement, after the well ceremony."

Six days went by. On the following day, a procession of women, with henna painted on their palms and long scarves draping their heads and bosoms, escorted the young mother to the village well. The new parent was so shrouded in veils that not an inch of her person could be seen; the baby too, in the arms of one of her companions, was tightly swaddled. The ladies circled the well, singing blessings to the newborn, while the mother leaning against a companion perambulated around the watery opening. She appeared weak and took faltering steps, clinging to the arms of her friends; she knew that any sign of strength on her part would only cause a jealous person to cast an evil eye on her child and had heard of tales where babies had been left lifeless overnight, the blood drained from their bodies through supernatural means.

The women returned from the ceremony and placed the baby in a cot on the front porch by her grandmother. During the next few weeks the household fell into its usual routines, the youngest swinging on her cot by her grandma by day and at night being tucked to sleep by her own mother.

Bursting with curiosity, the village girls and boys arrived daily to look at the newborn. "She is so beautiful," "Let me take her in my arms," the children said. Some of them came laden with red flowers while others brought rock-like sweets.

Old Bhuri Bai, aghast at the throng of children congregated at the front porch, spent all her waking hours in an agony of apprehension, lest a child poke the baby in the eye or attempt to feed her hard candy. She felt fiercely protective, though in her saner moments she questioned the wisdom of having so many girls. Her immediate extended family now totaled six daughters and a son. Where in the world would they find the dowry for each of them? They were of proud Rajput descent, and to marry into a fine family, the wedding portions for the girls would have to be majestic. Her sons were quite comfortably off, but the dowries were sure to bankrupt them.

Kushal came out to the porch and smiled down at his sleeping month-old niece. "This little child is the most beautiful among them; she is like a lotus flower. We should name her Padmini after the flower, and queen."

His mother sat at her spinning wheel a small distance away. "You always say that at the birth of each girl. Each one of them is a Padmini to you. For our six Padminis we have to corral six

Bhim Singhs. Where do you think you will find suitable mates for them? And how are we going to pay for them?"

Santosh joined them and stood by his daughter's crib. "We have to protect our Padminis from Ala-ud-dins!"

The baby woke up with a cry. Her uncle bent down, cradled her in his arms and rocked her. "Nowadays we need have no fear of Ala-ud-dins." He turned to his mother. "So what if there are six girls, what does it matter? Why do you keep bringing up the subject again and again?"

The old woman knitted her brow and gave a fierce glare. "You are fond of your niece, she is a darling no doubt, but we will all pay a heavy price for it in the future. You should hear what the people in our village are saying. Why, just the other day at the well, Ganeshi Bai gave me quite an earful. She told the others that I had lied and informed several people that this baby was a boy. That was a complete untruth. You should have heard her taunts at our having so many daughters to marry off."

The two brothers' faces turned grave and they looked at their mother in silence.

Kushal placed the child back in her crib with care. "Nowadays, people don't think of things like that. Why do you even bother to talk to such people? Whether we have sons or daughters is entirely our affair. It is no one else's business."

The newborn smiled and gurgled in her sleep. Her uncle forgot his annoyance at his fellow villagers, kneeled over the cot and ran a finger along her cheeks. "She is Padmini Bai. She is our Princess Padmini and will be Queen Padmini one day."

Another month went by and as the baby grew, a virulent form of typhoid struck the village with a stark suddenness. In cottage after cottage, both children and adults were felled by the disease. Soon after, an epidemic struck again, this time of the dreaded smallpox. The surviving villagers made regular offerings to the goddess of smallpox, Shitala Devi, crying out to her "Mata", "Phool Mata", or "Chhoti Mata", "Please bless us with longevity".

The illnesses that swept the village seemed to have sidestepped Bhuri Bai's home. During those dire weeks, the old woman watched her grandchildren fearfully, raking their skins with her eyes for any signs of reddened protuberances. She was fond of them all, her grandson who would carry on the family name, and even her granddaughters, Godaveri, Ganga, Janaki, Yamuna and Gauri. The girls were all so pretty, with delicate features and glowing complexions, and though they would cost a fortune in dowries in the future, she gave not a shred of thought to that. It was the baby, however, she looked askance at. She thanked God for having left her family unscathed.

During the afternoons, as she poured oil or molten butter on the girls' hair and braided it with ribbons, she told them time-honored folk tales, her favorites being 'The Golden Corn-Cob' and 'The Prince and the Peasant Girl'. Historical incidents too mingled with the stories and anecdotes of King Hanbir and Queen Kamalavati, and the murder of Princess Krishnakumari by milk laced with opium rolled off her tongue with ease.

"Poison? Why Grandma? You mean Princess Krishnakumari really died? Who gave her the poison, her father or her uncle? Why did they kill her?" asked twelve-year-old Godaveri.

All the girls, their eyes wide with fright, gazed up at their grandmother.

"Why do you think? She was a pure-blooded Rajput, a king's daughter. In such a family, you cannot have too many girls; they are a grave responsibility. It is a matter of family honor. No doubt she had sinned in her previous life." Bhuri Bai pursed her lips and fell silent and her glance fell upon the baby. There was no question; she was indeed a beauty. Her uncle was right; she was as attractive as her legendary namesake.

Godaveri, on the threshold of womanhood, stared in a wondering fashion at her grandmother, fear lurking in the depths of her eyes. The epic tales from the Ramayana and the Mahabharata, or the Arabian Nights were more palatable than these stories of wanton murder. "You mean to say that even the queens were burned alive?"

Kushal came to his mother's room as winter approached. "I plan on leaving for town early tomorrow morning. They have called me for some further training, but I will not be gone long, only about ten to twelve days. Later, they might send me elsewhere, but not right now. The crops will not be ready for harvest for quite some time, so my absence for a few days will not hurt our farms. Santosh will follow me later as he has some business affairs to settle in town. So, I leave you in charge of your grandson and six granddaughters. Your daughters-in-law will tend to the house and kitchen."

He smiled and knelt by the cot and lifted his sleeping niece in his arms and rocked her. "I will miss my Padmini. By the time I return, she will be even more beautiful. If I am delayed for any reason, I will not even be able to recognize her when I return."

Hearing his voice, his daughter, son and nieces gathered around him and barraged him with myriad requests.

"Can you please bring me a rag doll?"

"I want little wooden dolls please!"

"A complete toy cooking set and plates for me, uncle!"

The boy smiled up at his father. "I want a shining new toy motor car which travels faster than the wind!"

A few days later, Santosh left too, since as village headman he had to oversee sundry disputes at the courthouse in town. The epidemics that had swept the countryside with a terrifying intensity had vanished. The crisp wintry air brought a rosy flush to the children's cheeks; the buffalo's milk, clarified butter and frothy yogurt drinks strengthened their bones and the youngsters thrived on a daily diet of curried vegetables and whole wheat chapati.

All her granddaughters were true images of the Goddess Gangauri, and like their mothers they would blossom into great beauties, thought Bhuri Bai as she half-dozed in the evenings after sipping her sherbet with the customary dash of opium.

During the day, from time to time, she would rest her palm on her grandchildren's backs, checking to see if they had any fever as the weather was getting colder. No, their temperature was normal, and there was nary a cough among them. She stooped over the sleeping baby, marveling at the resilience of the child.

The next day, she gave orders to her daughters-in-law that her older son's wife was to preside over the kitchen in the mornings while the new mother rested, and only later in the day was the younger woman to cook their evening meal and leave her baby in the care of the grandmother. Their husbands away, the two ladies fell into the altered routine, though from time to time the elder stole a puzzled glance at her mother-in-law. From dawn to dusk, the wives, in turn, ground whole wheat, barley and millet on their stone grinder, pounded spices to a pulp and made flat breads by the dozen for every meal.

Some days later, Kushal and Santosh returned from their trips; they had taken longer than anticipated. It was well after midday when Santosh walked up to the gate, almost weighed down by the sack of parcels on his back; he was in high spirits as the disputes had been resolved with success. Kushal unlatched the gate and entered the courtyard laden with gifts, and in one hand, he carried an enormous red rattle. The children ran up and gathered around their father and uncle.

A smiling Kushal strode towards the cradle that stood on the porch, clutching the toy for his niece. The crib was empty. "Where is our Princess Padmini? Is she indoors?"

His mother, sitting at the far end of the porch, made no answer. A sudden wail from the kitchen caught his ears. His quick eyes swept over the faces of his son, daughter and nieces. They seemed subdued. His son stood by the sack of toys, making no attempt to undo the parcels, while the girls blinked back tears. His wife and sister-in-law leaned by the kitchen door, tears coursing down their cheeks.

He dropped down on a stool and stared at the empty crib. Beneath his turban, his eyes reddened and tears fell onto his curled moustache, the rattle still in his hand.

Santosh, his face a mask of anguish, went and sat down beside his mother in silence.

"When did she die?" Kushal asked.

The baby's mother stifled a sob. "Five days ago. She died a week after you left."

"What happened to her? What kind of illness did she have?" the father said.

The grandmother spoke. "Oh, nothing at all. One day her body seemed just a little warm, that's all."

The two men looked at their mother. "Did you try and get some medicine?"

"Neither of you were here. Who was there to go get medicine? We womenfolk cannot simply leave the house and go to the bazaar. Besides, the child had only a mild fever. She died rather suddenly."

Kushal gazed outdoors at the fields shimmering in the sun; then strode indoors.

Dinner was a solemn meal; conversation, limited at the best of times, was non-existent that evening. After a purple-hued sunset, darkness descended with astonishing rapidity. The children went to bed, while their mothers occupied themselves with their remaining chores in the kitchen before retiring for the night.

A stunned Santosh lay in his room, staring at the ceiling.

Kushal entered his mother's room. "Your worries are over."

Bhuri Bai gave her son a strange look. "Sri Ramji gave us the child and He took her back to Him." She wiped her eyes with the back of her hand.

"Yes, Sri Ramji has taken her. You gave her a bit too much opium isn't that so?"

The old woman twisted one end of her long scarf. "Do you think that this is the first time I have given sleeping aids to the children? Who looks after the brood when their mothers are busy in the kitchen and you men are out in the fields all day? Half the time you are away on training with the army and Santosh is busy settling disputes for the entire village. Do you believe that these children, healthy and active as they are, would fall asleep by themselves as quickly as they do if I didn't help things along with a dash of narcotic?"

Her son paced the room for a while, then walked to the door. His breathing uneven, he half-turned his head and looked out; in the darkness he saw the outline of the empty crib that had served all the newborns in their extended family.

He looked away and faced his mother. "Yes, I know that. You have been worrying over this for a long time haven't you?"

The woman's eyes widened, and she drew in her breath but said nothing.

Kushal's voice broke. "But since she was a girl, you gave her a dollop too much, didn't you?"

His mother arranged her pillows but remained silent. She pushed aside her glass of water and knocked it over; she grabbed a thin shawl and wiped the spill, her face expressionless. She smoothed her bed sheets and laid out the blankets. Without glancing up, she bent her head and blew out the candle.

Kushal stepped out and stumbled in the darkness, past the crib and back to his room.

Two Women

Sepoy Pishima

The homeowner, seated on a stone bench inside the walled courtyard, cleaned his teeth with care. A servant stood nearby with a tray-load of glasses brimming with water. The barber, his box of shaving creams and brushes beside him sat with towel in hand, ready to provide the daily shave. The usual visitors had streamed in through the front gate at daybreak and loitered by the entrance to the courtyard; some had come from the more remote villages in search of jobs while others sought pecuniary aid.

His ablutions finished, the master of the house turned his attention to the audience. At that moment, a tall woman swept in and, pressing her palms together in greeting, murmured, "Namaste." Dark-skinned, hair cropped short, lean to the point of being gaunt, her demeanor was mannish, though her attire feminine. A severe bout with smallpox had clearly not left the visitor unscathed. Her wrists, throat and earlobes were bare. She wore stout silver clasps around the ankles, resembling those of a man's rather than the more feminine anklets. She had a ten-year-old boy with a turban perched on his head in tow, who clutched a sword in its bejeweled sheath; dwarfed by the weapon, the child stood at attention.

The householder gave them a questioning glance.

The woman made her obeisance once again, while her eyes swept across the assembled company. Her air of unease was palpable. At a gesture from the property owner, the group dispersed and congregated by the far wall to await their turn.

"What do you need?" The gentleman asked.

She strode forward, holding the stripling by the hand, and then lifted his headgear and placed it on the ground along with the sword. "We want your help, and seek refuge."

She drew the boy forward. "This is my nephew. His mother and younger siblings are waiting around the corner behind your house. My brother has been dead three years, and his widow is very young. He was a zamindar in our village and owned considerably more than a hundred acres of fertile land, farmed by workers on our estate. We also had eight wells. But now, some of our relatives are trying to cheat my nephews of their rightful inheritance. They have already begun encroaching on our property holdings. We have no one in our extended family whom we can trust. And…"

She faltered, her eyes swam and voice broke, but she recovered her poise. "My sister-in-law is beautiful and has no experience in managing farmland. If we do not give in to their wishes, they are threatening to molest her. We know that they have been conspiring with unsavory men to destroy the honor of our family. The house we occupy at present has mud-brick walls and a thatched roof. They could set fire to it at any time, or they could scale the flimsy wooden fence surrounding our home and attack her while she is asleep.

"I have no source of help other than to come to you, an upstanding Bengali gentleman in town. I dare not approach anyone in our village for fear that they, too, might be easily bribed by our unscrupulous relatives. At your home, my sister-in-law will be safe. If you will allow her and the children temporary shelter, she will do any housework that you require."

The speaker pointed to the turban and sword which lay at the man's feet. "I am leaving these symbols of our Rajput heritage in the hope that you will allow my brother's widow sanctuary."

The guardian twisted the end of her filmy scarf. "I am anxious for the young woman's safety and need to get them all away from our village. The reputation of our entire lineage is at stake. If they succeed in harming her, our family will lose all standing in the community. I will return and discuss matters with our lawyer and we will also appreciate any advice from you."

She wiped her tears, and gazed at the seated gentleman with both fire and entreaty in her eyes. "Keep her as your maid. She can grind wheat for you, look after small children, do all the dusting and mopping, but of course, won't wash any dirty dishes. My relative is not to be seen in public, nor will she go to the bazaar for household shopping and most importantly, is never to speak to any of your menservants. If you can find a small room in your mansion, they can all stay there. Have her perform all the tasks that you would of your maids, although none of us have ever sullied our hands with menial work."

The homeowner remained silent. The list of domestic tasks that the young lady was willing to do was long, but the jobs that were far beneath her dignity were even more numerous.

"May I bring them over to meet you? They are waiting behind the walled compound of your house, Babuji."

He inclined his head.

The aunt strode around to the back of the residence and returned with her brother's widow and brood.

A woman, a long scarf enveloping her face and bosom, walked forward. Her arms, all the way up to the elbows, gleamed with clasps and bangles; necklaces with gold lockets glinted through the filmy veil. A jewel-studded waistband or *mekhla* anchored the skirt, while her feet were weighted with three or four rows of silver anklets. Balancing a little girl on her hip, she bowed in silent greeting.

She was very thin and young, the man observed to himself. He also noticed that her hands and feet were devoid of the floral henna or *mehndi* patterns displayed by married women.

"Yes, they can stay here in the women's section, and no doubt some housework can be assigned, but what kind of wages is she expecting?"

The aunt gave a shy smile. "Since you are being so kind as to offer them a home, and as my sister-in-law is willing to do chores for your family, any remuneration you offer will be gladly accepted. They know that they have to stay here until I can wrest back control of our property. In my brother's time, we had a large staff to wait on us, Babuji. We are now forced to stoop to domestic service. I do know, however, that they will be safe here."

The patriarch dispatched a servant to escort the entire family to the interior of the home. He turned his head towards the house and called out, "Is anyone there?"

His wife or daughter usually sat by the windows that were covered by wrought iron latticework, reading or sewing by the sunlight that filtered in.

"I am here," Roma said.

"You remember that large room where we store grain? Tell the servants to clear out the bags of fodder for the horses and cows and keep them elsewhere. Have them sweep the area thoroughly, so that the young woman and her children can stay there. The bins of rice and wheat can remain. I am coming indoors to have my breakfast and will discuss the whole situation with you and your mother."

The father went indoors and sat cross-legged on the low wooden *piri* laid out in the dining room. His widowed daughter brought out the steaming tea kettle and placed it on the spotless floor before him. Brass platters of puffed fried breads, or *luchis*, curried vegetables and sweetmeats lay arrayed in front. His wife poured the tea.

The provider looked at his offspring. "Has the woman found the lodgings to her liking?"

"Yes, she has. The place is being cleared and scrubbed clean."

He glanced at his wife and his lips quivered. "A damsel in distress has come to seek your bountiful aid and has indicated that she would like to earn her keep for however long it may be. But the lady has stated that she will not scrub utensils, nor venture outdoors under any circumstances; therefore, the question of sending her on errands to the bazaar does not even arise. Neither will she wash any of your saris. Rather like Gobra's mother in *Devi Choudhurani*."

Then he turned to his daughter. "However, she will look after your children, clean your vegetarian kitchen, and grind wheat for the entire household. Warn the menservants not to wander near their room, or even as much as glance in her direction. The aunt has a military temper and is the self-appointed guardian of that extended family. If she felt that their honor was in any way tarnished, her displeasure would rival that of an angry snake."

He faced his spouse again. "Did you get a chance to meet the visitor?"

"No, I was supervising in the kitchen. How does this person expect to remain cloistered and still work in our house? Servants are all over the place."

The husband laughed. "She won't exactly provide labor in the sense we understand. The lady is, after all, an aristocrat. Didn't you see her necklaces and bangles? And as for *purdah,* she will maintain her own seclusion; didn't you observe the long veils?" He rose and left the room in haste.

The mother looked at her daughter and gave a sniff. "Every woman wears loads of jewelry in these parts. All the maids and even many of the female sweepers wear if not gold, then silver or some other metal. Mere adornments don't indicate social rank. Besides, how can she do the job and still remain secluded? Although I am willing to provide assistance, I have no patience for such airs and graces."

Roma gave a grimace and walked towards the door of the storeroom. "She is very selective about tasks and moreover, we have to keep her hidden from our own male servants."

The visitor, her face now unveiled and with tears flowing, clasped her relative's hands. Roma glimpsed a painted tin trunk, a basket of cookware, pillows and bedrolls, all scattered on a reed mat. The boy's sword lay nearby, whilst the children hovered near their mother.

The aunt rubbed her own eyes. "You and my niece and nephews will be safe. No man can threaten you here, in Babuji's house. With our lawyer's help, we will get back our property."

She saw Roma in the doorway and once again conveyed her thanks by joining her palms together in a namaste, then bent down and hugged the children. "I will come and visit you all as often as I can."

The mother went to the door and bade farewell. "Come and see us again soon, Baiji."

It fell upon the daughter of the house to show the aristocrat her chores; in fact, her father had issued strict orders that no mere maid was to instruct the young lady in household duties. They both walked in silence around the many rooms, the Rajput woman still veiled, but her head covering was no longer down to the waist, but hung just by the forehead.

"What is your name?" Roma said.

"What do you need to know that for? Just call me Dhanji's mother or Dhanpal Singh's mother."

"Why can't you tell me your name? 'Dhanpal Singh's mother' is quite a mouthful."

The newcomer's eyes clouded with suspicion; only harlots were addressed by their names. Her bosom heaved and she fidgeted with her bangles. "I am Kamalabai, but please never call me that before your domestics. If you do, then your male servants will learn it and that is indeed a grievous offence to my clan. Respectable ladies remain nameless."

Roma sighed; the children's aunt too had displayed flamboyant gestures.

She guided the woman from room to room. "All right, Dhanji's mother, your first task is to grind about seven pounds of wheat today; the cook will make flatbreads for the entire household. Let me weigh out some for you. You are also to do the same amount of barley. We keep dogs you know, and they eat bread made from that grain along with chunks of meat. Please mop this kitchen which is used exclusively for vegetarian cuisine. Meat and fish are prepared at a separate location which you need not enter. When you have finished, please dust our bedrooms."

Kamalabai wrapped the scarf around her head and face baring only one eye as she took in the details of the spacious apartments. At her every footfall, there sounded the subtle clink of silver anklets and, at each movement, the necklaces glittered.

Roma left the woman to her chores and groused to herself as she walked down the corridor. "She dresses like a princess, wants to work as a maid, all the while promenading regally around our house." Recalling her father's admonishments, she flushed.

Kamalabai finished cleaning the rooms and returned to the storeroom which was to be home to her family for weeks if not months. She looked at the measured amounts of grain by the stone grinder in a corner and frowned. "After I have ground the wheat into flour, where will I make chapatis for my family? When will my children eat?"

Roma smiled. "If you want to make your bread in the sheltered courtyard right outside your room, you may. Or if you wish, you can use the huge charcoal burners in the kitchen when our cook has finished preparing our midday meal. If your kids are very hungry, why don't you put together a make-shift stove outdoors with bricks or large stones and prepare them?"

Unused to taking orders, Kamalabai stood immobile, her head inclined, and beneath the scowl, her eyes glistened.

Were they tears of anger or shame, wondered Roma. "I will tell our cook to provide you with lentil porridge and curried vegetables. Everyone receives vegetarian dishes from that kitchen, so please help yourself. Make your flatbreads now and I hope your children will enjoy their meal. When they have finished their lunch, you can start grinding wheat. We will only need it later in the day to make chapatis for dinner." Roma paused, and gave her companion a curious look. "How will you be able to work while wearing all that jewelry? Aren't they heavy? They must weigh at least ten to fifteen pounds."

"I used to have heaps more. During my husband's last illness, I had to sell off a great deal to pay for his medical care. When we fell on hard times, I had to dispose of a few more pieces. Now there is only a mere fraction left.

"Although I am widowed and should, by custom, wear few adornments, my sister-in-law advised me to put on everything when we left our house this morning in case they got stolen. We are much safer now in your home. Your father, Babuji, has been so kind in allowing us to stay here. I will lock up the jewels in my box tonight."

The training of Kamalabai began in earnest. It was easy enough to show a maid her chores, but teaching an aristocrat household duties was quite another matter, not the least of it being her incessant demand for being shielded from the prying eyes of servants. The children needed to be fed at their appointed mealtimes; any request was met with knitted brows and eyes darkened with anger as though amazed at the sheer effrontery of the speaker. Later, her demeanor would change in the stark realization of her new status, and only then would she deign to perform the task at hand. Murmurs arose among the servants. Disgruntled domestics could add to their household worries, so the mistress of the manor strove hard to maintain a semblance of order and serenity.

One evening, the two ladies of the house were invited to a relative's home, which was a short distance from their kitchen door through the back alleys. Strict *purdah* rules were maintained in Rajasthan where women did not venture along the main roads from their front entrances.

Roma walked to the storeroom and found Kamalabai mending a quilt by the light of an oil lamp while her offspring lay asleep on the mattress. "Dhanji's mother, we are going out and will return at eleven o'clock at night. Will you please do your sewing in my children's room? I have only just put them down to sleep, and they might wake up suddenly and start crying, so if you were there it might help."

Kamalabai's mouth hung open, as though amazed that a mother could even contemplate an evening out, leaving her progeny behind.

Roma tapped her foot and waited for a reply. There was none. "I will go and change my clothes. Will you come now?"

"And what about my own kids? Are they to lie all by themselves here?"

"They are sound asleep. You can come back from time to time to look in on them."

The new maid's eyes flashed defiance. "If your children need watching over, so do mine."

Roma drew in her breath and gripped the door knob till her knuckles whitened. The seconds and then minutes ticked by, but in the pregnant silence that ensued, Kamalabai's unceasing fingers flew over the quilt.

The next day at breakfast, Roma complained to her parents.

The mother concurred. "If we cannot even go out at night as occasion demands, of what use is such help? If she has chosen to work, then she must do the job required and not act like a princess."

The father finished his meal. He took a sip of tea and replaced the cup on the saucer. "What did she say? If your children cannot be left alone, then neither can hers?"

Roma's frowns vanished and she smiled. "I said that she could check on her kids from time to time. They were fast asleep, so I did not want to disturb them."

He gave a chuckle. "She is the daughter of a Rajput, not a Daroga, and is of proud heritage. Her manner and demeanor will always be that of an aristocrat. You must not let that annoy you. Is she going to obey you like a mere nanny or maid? The mother obviously didn't want to leave the toddlers by themselves. Didn't you know that Rajputs have a family name of Singh? Singh means lion. Lionesses are very protective of their cubs."

Roma's head jerked up and her eyes widened.

The mother gave a start. "The Mahabharata seems to be unfolding before our very eyes. Is Dhanji's mother our Draupadi in distress?"

The man's laughter rang out. "Almost, almost. She is certainly Draupadi, sans the five Pandavas. Only Bhim isn't here to protect her virtue. The sister-in-law, however, can easily take on the role of Bhim. The young lady has never done a hand's turn in her entire life. She doesn't even know the meaning of the word work.'"

Weeks expanded into months. The aunt visited from time to time and kept her benefactor informed about the progress of their legal affairs. Kamalabai, by this time, had grown accustomed to the ways of the household and her older boy assisted in various tasks. She appeared less concerned with real or imagined assaults on her modesty and the perpetual demand for seclusion had lessened; she felt safe. Meanwhile the servants had dubbed the aunt "Sepoy Baiji" or "Soldier Lady".

One morning, a carriage creaked up to the front gate. The paint had peeled off in a number of places and there were deep scratches on its sides. Resembling a chariot with the windows of the contraption covered in faded cloth, it might have leapt out of the pages of the ancient epic, the Mahabharata. Pulled by two oxen, it rumbled to a stop. The aunt descended from the conveyance with slow dignity. She was shrouded in veils and only her palms and sandal-clad feet were visible.

The doorman's mouth hung open. Some of the indoor servants came forward in bemused wonder. "Baiji, what has happened? Why are you wearing a veil today?"

The woman smiled, but said nothing. She entered the inner courtyard where the barber was giving the lord of the manor his daily shave. The visitor did not greet him with the customary gesture of namaste with palms folded, but knelt before him and bent her forehead low till it touched the ground and then rose. She appeared thinner and somehow softened.

He glanced at her, a questioning smile on his freshly lathered face.

Her eyes glistened. "We have finally been able to regain our land, thanks to you. You allowed my brother's widow and their children a safe haven. Who else would have protected her? We can now leave in peace, their honor untarnished."

"Were you able to get back your entire property?"

"Yes, nearly all. They, however, destroyed much of our arable land by turning it into pasture for their cows and then they set our granary on fire."

She walked indoors and approached Roma's mother. "Without your help, we would never have succeeded. In your villa, in the midst of so many men, was I able to safely leave my brother's widow. Please accept my deepest gratitude, I have come to take them home today."

Kamalabai, upon hearing a familiar voice, dropped the broom and ran and clasped her relative in a tearful embrace. She hurried back and completed the sweeping, and then left to take a bath. Afterwards, she clothed the children in brocaded finery, and placed turbans on the boys' heads. Dressed in an ankle-length skirt, an embroidered blouse and a veil edged in gold, she, along with her offspring, moved towards the mistress of the manse. Gone was her petulant pride. The sojourner bowed and took leave, murmuring, "Namaste", and breathed thanks in a scarcely audible whisper.

She walked to the kitchen, her anklets tinkling, and bade farewell to the Brahmin cook who had provided them with their daily fare of lentil soup and curried vegetables. Her eyes moist, she turned to the many retainers she had shunned and said goodbye.

Through the servants' grapevine, word flew fast about the family's wealth and jewels. Some whispered that the income from their estate or *jaigir* was two thousand rupees, while others said that it was five thousand or more.

The doubters among them sniffed. "Didn't you see their broken-down wagon? They are merely farm folk putting on airs."

The two women, their faces swathed in veils, walked out of the inner courtyard, and out to the gate. Behind them marched the children, the elder boy sporting his ancestral sword. They all climbed in and the carriage lurched forward. It rolled on the paved roads of the city and, by late afternoon, creaked along the rutted country lanes, past the fields of corn, pearl millet and barley in a storm of fiery dust.

Through the window grille, Dhanji's mother and aunt gazed at the distant fields as questions gnawed at their brains. How much of the property had been destroyed? Was the store house completely burnt down? These concerns vanished as they neared their home and relief washed over them at the thought of reclaiming their ancestral lands.

Acknowledgments

My thanks go to the original trustees: Anima Ray, Anjali Chatterjee and Ashoka Gupta who gave me permission to translate this collection. I am indebted to Shrikhandath Narayan Menon and Kasturi Gupta Menon, who organized my trips to visit historic sites in Rajasthan for research purposes. My deep appreciation goes to John Robert Egan who has helped me with computer work. A heartfelt thanks to Ritabari Roychowdhury, Siddhartha Kumar Gupta, Aparajita Mukherjee Nanda, Narayani Gupta, Parijat Mazumder and Srirupa Dasgupta for their help.